A Call to Prayer
&
How Readest Thou?

John Charles Ryle

A Call to Prayer and How Readest Thou?

Copyright © 2018 Indo-European Publishing

The present edition is a reproduction of previous publication of this work. Minor typographical errors may have been corrected without note, however, for an authentic reading experience the spelling, punctuation, and capitalization have been retained from the original text.

ISBN: 978-1-60444-945-7

CONTENTS

A CALL TO PRAYER 1

HOW READEST THOU? 39

Salvation Found Only In The Bible 39
No Other Like The Book Bible 42
Such Important Matter 48
Effects Of The Bible On Humanity 56
No Other Book Can Do As Much 64
Nothing As Misused Or Neglected 70
The Only Rule For Questions On Doctrine 79
The Book Of God's Servants 86
The Only Book Which Comforts In The Final
Hours 91
A Warning To Those Who Do Not Read 97
Practical Advice For Reading The Bible 100

A CALL TO PRAYER

" MEN OUGHT ALWAYS TO PRAY." Luke 18: 1.
"THAT MEN PRAY EVERYWHERE."
1 TIM. 2.1.

I HAVE a question to offer you. It is contained in three words, Do you pray?

The question is one that none but you can answer. Whether you attend public worship or not, your minister knows. Whether you attend public worship or not your minister knows. Whether you have family prayers in your house or not, your relations know. But whether you pray in private or not, is a matter between yourself and God.

I beseech you in all affection to attend to the subject I bring before you. Do not say that my question is too close. If your heart is right in the sight of God, there is nothing in it to make you afraid. Do not turn off my question by replying that you say your prayers. It is one thing to say your prayers and another to pray. Do not tell me that my question is unnecessary. Listen to me for a few minutes, and I will show you good reasons for asking it.

I. I ask whether you pray, because *prayer is absolutely needful to a man's salvation.*

I say, absolutely needful, and I say so advisedly. I am not speaking now of infants or idiots. I am not settling the state

1

of the heathen. I know that where little is given, there little will be required. I speak especially of those who call themselves Christians, in a land like our own. And of such I say, no man or woman can expect to be saved who does not pray.

I hold salvation by grace as strongly as any one. I would gladly offer a free and full pardon to the greatest sinner that ever lived. I would not hesitate to stand by his dying bed, and say, "Believe on the Lord Jesus Christ even now, and you shall be saved." But that a man can have salvation without asking for it, I cannot see in the Bible. That a man will receive pardon of his sins, who will not so much as lift up his heart inwardly, and say, "Lord Jesus, give it to me," this I cannot find. I can find that nobody will be saved by his prayers, but I cannot find that without prayer anybody will be saved.

It is not absolutely needful to salvation that a man should read the Bible. A man may have no learning, or be blind, and yet have Christ in his heart. It is not absolutely needful that a man should hear public preaching of the gospel. He may live where the gospel is not preached, or he may be bedridden, or deaf. But the same thing cannot be said about prayer. It is absolutely needful to salvation that a man should *pray*.

There is no royal road either to health or learning. Princes and kings, poor men and peasants, all alike must attend to the wants of their own bodies and their own minds. No man can eat, drink, or sleep, by proxy. No man can get the alphabet learned for him by another. All these are things which everybody must do for himself, or they will not be done at all.

Just as it is with the mind and body, so it is with the soul. There are certain things absolutely needful to the soul's health and well – being. Each must attend to these things for himself. Each must repent for himself. Each must apply to Christ for himself. And for himself each must speak to God and pray. You must do it for yourself, for by nobody else can it be done.

To be prayerless is to be without God, without Christ, without grace, without hope, and without heaven. It is to be in the road to hell. Now can you wonder that I ask the question, DO YOU PRAY?

II. I ask again whether you pray, because *a habit of prayer is one of the surest marks of a true Christian.*

All the children of God on earth are alike in this respect. From the moment there is any life and reality about their religion, they pray. Just as the first sign of life in an infant when born into the world, is the act of breathing, so the first act of men and women when they are born again, is *praying*.

This is one of the common marks of all the elect of God, "They cry unto him day and night." Luke 18:1. The Holy Spirit, who makes them new creatures, works in them the feeling of adoption, and makes them cry, "Abba, Father." Rom. 8: 15. The Lord Jesus, when he quickens them, gives them a voice and a tongue, and says to them, "Be dumb no more." God has no dumb children. It is as much a part of their new nature to pray, as it is of a child to cry. They see

3

their need of mercy and grace. They feel their emptiness and weakness. They cannot do otherwise than they do. They *must* pray.

I have looked carefully over the lives of

God's saints in the Bible. I cannot find one of whose history much is told us, from Genesis to Revelation, who was not a man of prayer. I find it mentioned as a characteristic of the godly, that "they call on the Father," that "they call on the name of the Lord Jesus Christ." I find it recorded as a characteristic of the wicked, that "they call not upon the Lord." 1 Peter 1:17; 1 Cor. 1:2; Psa. 14:4.

I have read the lives of many eminent Christians who have been on earth since the Bible days. Some of them, I see, were rich, and some poor. Some were learned, and some unlearned. Some of them were Episcopalians, and some Christians of other names. Some were Calvinists, and some were Arminians. Some have loved to use a liturgy, and some to use none. But one thing, I see, they all had in common. They have all been *men of prayer*.

I study the reports of missionary societies in our own times. I see with joy that heathen men and women are receiving the gospel in various parts of the globe. There are conversions in Africa, in New Zealand, in Hindostan, in China. The people converted are naturally unlike one another in every respect. But one striking thing I observe at all the missionary stations: the converted people *always pray*.

I do not deny that a man may pray without heart and without sincerity. I do not for a moment pretend to say that the mere fact of a person's praying proves everything about his soul. As in every other part of religion, so also in this, there may be deception and hypocrisy.

But this I do say, that not praying is a clear proof that a man is not yet a true Christian. He cannot really feel his sins. He cannot love God. He cannot feel himself a debtor to Christ. He cannot long after holiness. He cannot desire heaven. He has yet to be born again. He has yet to be made a new creature. He may boast confidently of election, grace, faith, hope, and knowledge, and deceive ignorant people. But you may rest assured it is all vain talk *if he does not pray*.

And I say, furthermore, that of all the evidences of the real work of the Spirit, a habit of hearty private prayer is one of the most satisfactory that can be named. A man may preach from false motives. A man may write books and make fine speeches and seem diligent in good works, and yet be a Judas Iscariot. But a man seldom goes into his closet, and pours out his soul before God in secret, unless he is in earnest. The Lord himself has set his stamp on prayer as the best proof of a true conversion. When he sent Ananias to Saul in Damascus, he gave him no other evidence of his change of heart than this, "Behold, he prayeth" Acts 9: 11. '

I know that much may go on in a man's mind before he is brought to pray. He may have many convictions, desires, wishes, feelings, intentions, resolutions, hopes, and fears. But all these things are very uncertain evidences. They are to be found in ungodly people, and often come to nothing. In many a case they are not more lasting than the morning cloud and the dew that passeth away. A real, hearty prayer, flowing from a broken and contrite spirit, is worth all , these things put together.

5

I know that the only Spirit, who calls sinners from their evil ways, does in many instances lead them by very slow degrees to acquaintance with Christ. But the eye of man can only judge by what it sees. I cannot call any one justified until he believes. I dare not say that any one believes until he prays. I cannot understand a dumb faith. The first act of faith will be to speak to God, Faith is to the soul what life is to the body. Prayer is to faith what breath is to life. How a man can live and not breathe is past my comprehension, and how a man can believe and not pray is past my comprehension too.

Never be surprised if you hear ministers of the gospel dwelling much on the importance of prayer. This is the point we want to bring you to we want to know that you pray. Your views of doctrine may be correct. Your love of Protestantism may be warm and unmistakable. But still this may be nothing more than head knowledge and party spirit. We want to know whether you are actually acquainted with the throne of grace, and whether you can speak to God as well as speak about God.

Do you wish to find out whether you are a true Christian? Then rest assured that my question is of the very first importance Do YOU PRAY?

III. I ask whether you pray, because *there is no duty in religion so neglected as private prayer.*

We live in days of abounding religious profession. There are more places of public worship now than there ever were before. There are more persons attending them than there ever were before. And yet in spite of all this public religion, I believe there is a vast neglect of private prayer. It is one of those private transactions, between God and our souls which no eye sees, and therefore one which men are tempted to pass over and leave undone.

I believe that thousands *never utter a word of prayer at all.* They eat. They drink. They sleep. They rise. They go forth to their labor. They return to their homes. They breathe God's air. They see God's sun. They walk on God's earth. They enjoy God's mercies. They have dying bodies. They have judgment and eternity before them. But they *never speak to God.* They live like the beasts that perish. They behave like creatures without souls. They have not one word to say to Him in whose hand are their life and breath and all things, and from whose mouth they must one day receive their everlasting sentence. How dreadful this seems, but if the secrets of men were only known, how common.

I believe there are tens of thousands whose prayers are nothing hut a mere form, a set of words repeated by rote, without a thought about their meaning. Some say over a few hasty sentences picked up in the nursery when they were children. Some content themselves with repeating the Creed, forgetting that there is not a request in it. Some add the Lord's Prayer, but without the slightest desire that its solemn petitions may he granted.

Many, even of those who use good forms, mutter their prayers over after they have got into bed, or while they wash or dress in the morning. Men may think what they please, but they may depend upon it that in the sight of *God this is not praying*. Words said without heart are as utterly useless to our souls as the drum – beating of the poor heathen before their idols. Where there is no heart, there may be lip – work and tongue work, but there is nothing that God listens to; there is no prayer. Saul, I have no doubt, said many a long prayer before the Lord met him on the way to Damascus. But it was not till his heart was broken that the Lord said, "He prayeth."

Does this surprise you? Listen to me, and I will show you that I not speaking as I do without reason. Do you think that my assertions are extravagant and unwarrantable? Give me your attention, and I will soon show you that I am only telling you the truth.

Have you forgotten that it is *not natural* to any one to pray? "The carnal mind is enmity against God." The desire of man's heart is to get far away from God, and have nothing to do with him. His feeling towards him is not love, but fear. Why then should a man pray when he has no real sense of sin, no real feeling of spiritual wants, no thorough belief in unseen things, no desire after holiness and heaven? Of all these things the vast majority of men know and feel nothing. The multitude walk in the broad way. I cannot forget this. Therefore I say boldly, I believe that few pray.

Have you forgotten that it is not fashionable to pray? It is one of the things that many would be rather ashamed to own. There are hundreds who would sooner storm a breach or lead a forlorn hope, than confess publicly that they make a habit of prayer. There are thousands who, if obliged to sleep in the same room with a stranger, would lie down in bed without a prayer. To dress well, to go to theatres, to be thought clever and agreeable, all this is fashionable, but not to pray. I cannot forget this. I cannot think a habit is common which so many seem ashamed to own. I believe that few pray.

Have you forgotten *the lives that many live*? Can we really believe that people are praying against sin night and day, when we see them plunging into it? Can we suppose they pray against the world, when they are entirely absorbed and taken up with its pursuits? Can we think they really ask God for grace to serve him, when they do not show the slightest desire to serve him at all? Oh, no, it is plain as daylight that the great majority of men either ask nothing of God or *do not mean that they say* when they do ask, which is just the same thing. Praying and sinning will never live together in the same heart. Prayer will consume sin, or sin will choke prayer.

I cannot forget this, I look at men's lives. I believe that few pray.

Have you forgotten the deaths that many die? How many, when they draw near death, seem entirely strangers to God. Not only are they sadly ignorant of his gospel, but sadly wanting in the power of speaking to him. There is a terrible awkwardness and shyness in their endeavors to approach Him. They seem to be taking up a fresh thing. They appear as if they wanted an introduction to God, and as if they had never talked with him before. I remember having heard of a lady who was anxious to have a minister to visit her in her last illness. She desired that he would pray with her. He asked her what he should pray for. She did not know, and could not tell. She was utterly unable to name any one thing which she wished him to ask God for her soul. All she seemed to want was the form of a minister's prayers. I can quite understand this. Death – beds are great revealers of secrets. I cannot forget what I have seen of sick and dying people. This also leads me to believe that few pray.

I cannot see your heart. I do not know your private history in spiritual things. But from what I see in the Bible and in the world, I am certain I cannot ask you a more necessary question than that before you – Do YOU PRAY?

IV. I ask whether you pray, because *prayer is an act in religion to which there is great encouragement.*

There is everything on God's part to make prayer easy, if men will only attempt it. All things are ready on his side. Every objection is anticipated. Every difficulty is provided for. The crooked places are made straight and the rough places are made smooth. There is no excuse left for the prayerless man.

There is a *way* by which any man, however sinful and unworthy, may draw near to God the Father. Jesus Christ has opened that way by the sacrifice he made for us upon the cross. The holiness, and justice of God need not frighten sinners and keep them back. Only let them cry to God in the name of Jesus, only let them plead the atoning blood of Jesus, and they shall find God upon a throne of grace, willing and ready to hear. The name of Jesus is a never –

failing passport for our prayers. In that name a man may draw near to God with boldness, and ask with confidence. God has engaged to hear him. Think of this. Is not this encouragement?

There is *an Advocate* and Intercessor always waiting to present the prayers of those who come to God through him. That advocate is Jesus Christ. He mingles our prayers with the incense of his own almighty intercession. So mingled, they go up as a sweet savor before the throne of God. Poor as they are in themselves, they are mighty and powerful in the hand of our High Priest and Elder Brother. The bank – note without a signature at the bottom is nothing but a worthless piece of paper. The stroke of a pen confers on it all its value. The prayer of a poor child of Adam is a feeble thing in itself, but once endorsed by the hand of the Lord Jesus it availeth much. There was an officer in the city of Rome who was appointed to have his doors always open, in order to receive any Roman citizen who appointed to him for help. Just so the ear of the Lord Jesus is ever open to the cry of all who want mercy and grace. It is his office to help them. Their prayer is his delight. Think of this. Is not this encouragement?

There is *the Holy Spirit* ever ready to help our infirmities in prayer. It is one part of his special office to assist us in our endeavors to speak with God. We need not be cast down and distressed by the fear of not knowing what to say. The Spirit will give us words if we seek his aid. The prayers of the Lord's people are the inspiration of the Lord's Spirit, the work of the Holy Ghost who dwells within them as the

Spirit of grace and supplication. Surely the Lord's people may well hope to be heard. It is not they merely that pray, but the Holy Ghost pleading in them.

Reader think of this. Is not this encouragement?

There are exceeding great and precious promises to those who pray. What did the Lord Jesus mean when he spoke such words as these: Ask, and it shall be given you; seek, and ye shall find; knock, and it shall be opened unto you: for every one that asketh, receiveth; and he that seeketh, findeth; and to him that knocketh, it shall be opened." Matt: 7:7, 8. "All things whatsoever ye shall ask in prayer believing, ye shall receive." Matt. 21:22. "Whatsoever ye shall ask in my name, that will I do, that the Father may be glorified in the Son. If ye shall ask anything in my name, I will do it." John 14:13, 14. What did the Lord mean when he spoke the parables of The friend at midnight and The importunate widow? Luke 11:5; 18:1. Think over these passages. If this is not encouragement to pray, words have no meaning.

There are wonderful *examples* in Scripture of the power of prayer. Nothing seems to be too great, too hard, or too difficult for prayer to do. It has obtained things that seemed impossible and out of reach. It has won victories over fire, air, earth, and water. Prayer opened the Red sea. Prayer brought water from the rock and bread from heaven. Prayer made the sun stand still. Prayer brought fire from the sky on Elijah's sacrifice. Prayer turned the counsel of Ahithophel into foolishness. Prayer overthrew the army of Sennacherib. Well might Mary Queen of Scots say, "I fear John Knox's

12

prayers more than an army of ten thousand men." Prayer has healed the sick. Prayer has raised the dead. Prayer has procured the conversion of souls. "The child of many prayers," said an old Christian to Augustine's mother, "shall never perish." Prayer, pains, and faith can do anything. Nothing seems impossible when a man has the spirit of adoption. "Let me alone," is the remarkable saying of God to Moses, when Moses was about to intercede for the children of Israel; the Chaldee version has it, "Leave off praying." Exod. 32:10.

So long as Abraham asked mercy for Sodom, the Lord went on giving. He never ceased to give till Abraham ceased to pray. Think of this. Is not this encouragement?

What more can a man want to lead him to take any step in religion, than the things I have just told him about prayer? What more could be done to make the path to the mercy – seat easy, and to remove all Occasions of stumbling from the sinner's way? Surely if the devils in hell had such a door set open before them, they would leap for gladness, and make the very pit ring with joy.

But where will the man hide his head at last who neglects such glorious encouragements? What can possibly be said for the man who, after all, dies without prayer? Surely I may feel anxious that you should not be that man. Surely I may well ask – Do YOU PRAY?

V. I ask whether you pray, because *diligence in prayer is the secret of eminent holiness.*

Without controversy there is a vast difference among true

Christians. There is an immense interval between the foremost and the hindermost in the army of God.

They are all fighting the same good fight; but how much more valiantly some fight than others. They are all doing the Lord's work; but how much more some do than others. They are all light in the Lord; but how much more brightly some shine than others. They are all running the same race; but how much faster some get on than others. They all love the same Lord and Saviour; but how much more some love him than others. I ask any true Christian whether this is not the case. Are not these things so?

There are some of the Lord's people who seem *never able to get on* from the time of their conversion. They are born again, but they remain babes all their lives. You hear from thorn the same old experience. You remark in them the same want of spiritual appetite, the same want of interest in anything beyond their own little circle, which you remarked ten years ago. They are pilgrims, indeed, but pilgrims like the Gibeonites of old; their bread is always dry and mouldy, their shoes always old, and their garments always rent and torn. I say this with sorrow and grief; but I ask any real Christian, Is it not true?

There are others of the Lord's people who seem to be *always advancing*. They grow like the grass after rain; they increase like Israel in Egypt; they press on like Gideon, though sometimes faint, yet always pursuing. They are ever adding grace to grace, and faith to faith, and strength to strength. Every time you meet them their hearts seem larger, and their spiritual stature taller and stronger. Every year they appear to see more, and know more, and believe more, and feel more in their region. They not only have good works to prove the reality of their faith, but they are zealous of them. They not only do well, but they are unwearied in well – doing. They attempt great things, and they do great things. When they fail they try again, and when they fall they are soon up again. And all this time they think themselves poor, unprofitable servants, and fancy they do nothing at all. These are those who make religion lovely and beautiful in the eyes of all. They wrest praise even from the unconverted, and win golden opinions even from the selfish men of the world. It does one good to see, to be with, and to hear them. When you meet them, you could believe that like Moses, they had just come out from the presence of God. When you part with them you feel warmed by their company, as if your soul had been near a fire. I know such people are rare. I only ask. Are there not many such?

Now how can we account for the difference which I have just described? What is the reason that some believers are so much brighter and holier than others? I believe the difference, in nineteen cases out of twenty, arises from different habits about private prayer. I believe that those who are not eminently holy pray little, and those who are eminently holy pray much.

I dare say this opinion will startle some readers. I have little doubt that many look on eminent holiness as a kind of special gift, which none but a few must pretend to aim at. They admire it at a distance in books. They think it beautiful when they see an example near themselves. But as to its being a thing within the reach of any but a very few, such a notion never seems to enter their minds. In short, they consider it a kind of monopoly granted to a few favored believers, but certainly not to all.

Now I believe that this is a most dangerous mistake. I believe that spiritual as well as natural greatness depends in a high degree on the faithful use of means within everybody's reach. Of course I do not say we have a right to expect a miraculous grant of intellectual gifts; but this I do say, that when a man is once converted to God, his progress in holiness will be much in accordance with his own diligence in the use of God's appointed means. And I assert confidently that the principal means by which most believers have become great in the church of Christ, is the habit of diligent private prayer.

Look through the lives of the brightest and best of God's servants, whether in the Bible or not. See what is written of Moses and David and Daniel and Paul. Mark what is recorded of Luther and Bradford the Reformers. Observe what is related of the private devotions of Whitefield and Cecil and Venn and Bickersteth and M'Cheyne. Tell me of one of all the goodly fellowship of saints and martyrs, who has not had this mark most prominently – he was a wow of grayer. Depend upon it, prayer is power.

Prayer obtains fresh and continued outpourings of the Spirit. He alone begins the work of grace in a man's heart. He alone can carry it forward and make it prosper. But the good Spirit loves to be entreated. And those who ask most will have most of his influence.

Prayer is the surest remedy against the devil and besetting sins. That sin will never stand firm which is heartily prayed against. That devil will never long keep dominion over us which we beseech the Lord to cast forth. But then we must spread out all our case before our heavenly Physician, if he is to give us daily relief.

Do you wish to grow in grace and be a devoted Christian? Be very sure, if you wish it, you could not have a more important question than – Do YOU PRAY?

VI. I ask whether you pray, *because neglect of prayer is one great cause of backsliding*.

There is such a thing as going back in religion after making a good profession. Men may run well for a season, like the Galatians, and then turn aside after false teachers. Men may profess loudly while their feelings are warm, as Peter did, and then in the hour of trial deny their Lord. Men may lose their first love as the Ephesians did. Men may cool down in their zeal to do good, like Mark the companion of Paul. Men may follow an apostle for a season, and like Demas go back to the world. All these things men may do.

It is a miserable thing to be a backslider. Of all unhappy things that can befall a man, I suppose it is the worst. A stranded ship, a broken – winged eagle, a garden overrun with weeds, a harp without strings, a church in ruins, all these are sad sights, but a backslider is a sadder sight still. A wounded conscience – a mind sick of itself – a memory full of self – reproach – a heart pierced through with the Lord's arrows – a spirit broken with a load of inward accusation –

all this is a taste of hell. It is a hell on earth. Truly that saying of the wise man is solemn and weighty, "The backslider in heart shall be filled with his own ways." Prov. 14:14.

Now what is the cause of most backslidings? I believe, as a general rule, one of the chief causes is neglect of private prayer. Of course the secret history of falls will not be known till the last day. I can only give my opinion as a minister of Christ and a student of the heart. That opinion is, I repeat distinctly, that backsliding generally first begins with *neglect of private prayer.*

Bibles read without prayer; sermons heard without prayer; marriages contracted without prayer; journeys undertaken without prayer; residences chosen without prayer; friendships formed without prayer; the daily act of private prayer itself hurried over, or gone through without heart: these are the kind of downward steps by which many a Christian descends to a condition of spiritual palsy, or reaches the point where God allows him to have a tremendous fall.

This is the process which forms the lingering Lots, the unstable Samson's, the wife – idolizing Solomon's, the inconsistent Asas, the pliable Jehoshaphat's, the over – careful Martha's, of whom so many are to be found in the church of Christ. Often the simple history of such cases is this: they became *careless about private prayer.*

You may be very sure men fall in private long before they fall in public. They are backsliders on their knees long before they backslide openly in the eyes of the world, tike Peter, they first disregard the Lord's warning to watch and pray, and then like Peter, their strength is gone, and in the hour of temptation they deny their Lord.

The world takes notice of their fall, and scoffs loudly. But the world knows nothing of the real reason. The heathen succeeded in making a well – known Christian 'offer incense to an idol, by threatening him with a punishment worse than death. They then triumphed greatly at the sight of his cowardice and apostasy. But the heathen did not know the fact of which history informs us, that on that very morning he had left his bed – chamber hastily, and without finishing his usual prayers.

If you are a Christian indeed, I trust you will never be a backslider. But if you do not wish to be a backsliding Christian, remember the question I ask you: Do you peat?

VII. I ask, lastly, whether you pray because *prayer is one of the best means of happiness and contentment.*

We live in a world where sorrow abounds. This has always been its state since sin came m. There cannot be sin without sorrow. And until sin is driven out from the world, it is vain for any one to suppose he can escape sorrow.

Some without doubt have a larger cup of sorrow to drink than others. But few are to be found who lire long without sorrows or cares of one sort or another. Our bodies, our property, our families, our children, our relations, our servants, our friends, our neighbors, our worldly callings, each and all of these are fountains of care. Sicknesses, deaths, losses, disappointments, partings, separations, ingratitude, slander, all these are common things. "We cannot get through life without them. Some day or other they find us out. The greater are our affections the deeper are our afflictions, and the more we love the more we have to weep.

And what is the best means of cheerfulness in such a world as this? How shall we get through this valley of tears with least pain? I know no better means than the habit of *taking everything to God in prayer.*

This is the plain advice that the Bible gives, both in the Old Testament and the New. What says the psalmist? "Call upon me in the day of trouble, and I will deliver thee, and thou shalt glorify me." Psa. 50 : 15. "Cast thy burden upon the Lord, and he shall sustain thee: he shall never suffer the righteous to be moved." Psa. 55: 22. What says the apostle Paul? "Be careful for nothing; but in everything, by prayer and supplication with thanksgiving, let your requests be made known unto God: and the peace of God, which passeth all understanding shall keep your hearts and minds through Christ Jesus." Phil. 4: 6, 7. What says the apostle James: "Is any afflicted among you? Let him pray." Jas. 5:13.

This was the practice of all the saints whose history we have recorded in the Scriptures. This is what Jacob did when he feared his brother Esau. This is what Moses did when the people were ready to stone him in the wilderness. This is what Joshua did when Israel was defeated before the men of Ai. This is what David did when he was in danger at Keilah. This is what Hezekiah did when he received the letter from Sennacherib. This is what the church did when Peter was put in prison. This is what Paul did when he was cast into the dungeon at Philippi.

The only way to be really happy in such a world as this, is to be ever casting all our cares on God. It is trying to carry their own burdens which so often makes believers sad. If they will tell their troubles to God, he will enable them to bear them as easily as Samson did the gates of Gaza. If they are resolved to keep them to themselves, they will find one day that the very grasshopper is a burden.

There is a friend ever waiting to help us, if we will unbosom to him our sorrow – a friend who pitied the poor and sick and sorrowful, when he was upon earth – a friend who knows the heart of man, for he lived thirty – three years as a man among us – a friend who can weep with the weepers, for he was a man of sorrows and acquainted with grief – a friend who is able to help us, for there never was earthly pain he could not cure. That friend is Jesus Christ. The way to be happy is to be always opening our hearts to him. Oh .that we were all like that poor Christian negro who only answered, when threatened and punished, *"I must tell the Lord."*

Jesus can make those happy who trust him and call on him, whatever be their outward condition. He can give them peace of heart in a prison, contentment in the midst of poverty, comfort in the midst of bereavements, joy on the brink of the grave. There is a mighty fulness in him for all his believing members – a fulness that is ready to be poured out on every one that will ask in prayer. Oh that men would understand that happiness does not depend on outward circumstances, but on the state of the heart.

Prayer can lighten crosses for us, however heavy. It can

bring down to our side One who will help us to bear them. Prayer can open a door for us when our way seems hedged up. It (can bring down One who will say, "This is the way, walk in it." Prayer can let in a ray of hope when all our earthly prospects seem darkened. It can bring down One who will say, "I will never leave thee, nor forsake thee." Prayer can obtain relief for us when those we love most are taken away, and the world feels empty. It can bring down One who can fill the gap in our hearts with himself, and say to the waves within, "Peace; be still." Oh that men were not so like Hagar in the wilderness, blind to the well of living waters close beside them.

I want you to be happy. I know I cannot ask you a more useful question than this: Do YOU PRAY?

And now it is high time for me to bring this tract to an end. I trust I have brought before you things that will be seriously considered. I heartily pray God that this consideration may be blessed to your soul.

1. Let me speak a parting word TO THOSE WHO DO NOT PRAY. I dare not suppose that all who read these pages are praying people. If you are a prayerless person, suffer me to speak to you this day on God's behalf.

Prayerless reader, I can only warn you, but I do warn you most solemnly. I warn you that you are in a position of fearful danger. If you die in your present state, you are a lost soul. You will only rise again to be eternally miserable. I warn you that of all professing Christians you are most utterly without excuse. There is not a single good reason that you can show for living without prayer.

22

It is useless to say you *know not how to pray*. Prayer is the simplest act in all religion. It is simply speaking to God. It needs neither learning nor wisdom nor book – knowledge to begin it. It needs nothing but heart and will. The weakest infant can cry when he is hungry. The poorest beggar can hold out his hand for alms, and does not wait to find fine words. The most ignorant man will find something to say to God, if he has only a mind.

It is useless to say you have *no convenient place* to pray in. Any man can find a place private enough, if he is disposed. Our Lord prayed on a mountain; Peter on the housetop; Isaac in the field; Nathanael under the fig – tree; Jonah in the whale's belly. Any place may become a closet, an oratory, and a Bethel, and be to us the presence of God.

It is useless to say you *have no time*. There is plenty of time, if men will employ it. Time may be short, but time is always long enough for prayer. Daniel had the affairs of a kingdom on his hands, and yet he prayed three times a day. David was ruler over a mighty nation, and yet he says, "Evening and morning and at noon will I pray." Psa. 55 :17. When time is really wanted, time can always be found.

It is useless to say you *cannot pray till you have faith and a new heart*, and that you must sit still and wait for them. This is to add sin to sin. It is bad enough to be unconverted and going to hell. It is even worse to say, "I know it, but will not cry for mercy." This is a kind of argument for which there is no warrant in Scripture. "Call ye upon the Lord," says Isaiah, "while he is near." Isa. 55 :6. "Take with you words, and turn unto the Lord," says Hosea. Hos. 14 : 1. "Repent and pray," says Peter to Simon Magus. Acts 8:22. If you want faith and a new heart, go and cry to the Lord for them. The very attempt to pray has often been the quickening of a dead soul.

Oh, prayerless reader, who and what are you that you will not ask anything of God? Have you made a covenant with death and hell? Are you at peace with the worm and the fire? Have you no sins to be pardoned? Have you no fear of eternal torment? Have you no desire after heaven? Oh that you would awake from your present folly. Oh that you would consider your latter end. Oh that you would arise and call upon God. Alas, there is a day coming when many shall pray loudly, "Lord, Lord, open to us," but all too late; when many shall cry to the rocks to fall on them and the hills to cover them, who would never cry to God. In all affection, I warn you, beware lest this be the end of your soul. Salvation 'is very near you. Do not lose heaven for want of asking.

2. Let me speak TO THOSE WHO HAVE REAL DESIRES for SALVATION, but know not what steps to take, or where to begin. 1 cannot but hope that some readers may be in this state of mind, and if there be but one such I must offer him affectionate counsel.

In every journey there must be a first step. There must be a change from sitting still to moving forward. The journeyings of Israel from Egypt to Canaan were long and wearisome. Forty years pass away before, they crossed Jordan. Yet there was some one who moved first when they marched from Ramah to Succoth. When does a man really take his first step in coming out from sin and the world? He does it in the day when he first prays with his heart.

In every building the first stone must be laid, and the first blow must be struck. The ark was one hundred and twenty years in building. Yet there was a day when Noah laid his axe to the first tree he cut down to form it. The temple of Solomon was a glorious building. But there was a day when the first huge stone was laid deep in mount Moriah. When does the building of the Spirit really begin to appear in a man's heart? It begins, so far as we can judge, when he first pours out his heart to God in prayer.

If you desire salvation, and want to know what to do, I advise you to go this very day to the Lord Jesus Christ, in the first private place you can find, and earnestly and heartily entreat him in prayer to save your soul.

Tell him that you have heard that he receives sinners, and has said, "Him that Cometh unto me I will in nowise cast out." Tell him that you are" a poor vile sinner, and that you come to him on the faith of his own invitation. Tell him you put yourself wholly and entirely in his hands; that you feel vile and helpless, and hopeless in yourself: and that except he saves you, you have no hope of being saved at all. Beseech him to deliver you from the guilt, the power, and the consequences of sin. Beseech him to pardon you, and wash you in his own blood. Beseech him to give you a new heart, and plant the Holy Spirit in your soul. Beseech him to give you grace and faith, and will and power to be his disciple and servant from this day for ever. Oh, reader, go this very day, and tell these things to the Lord Jesus Christ, if you really are. in earnest about your soul.

Tell him in your own way, and your own words. If a doctor came to see you when sick, you could tell him where you felt pain. If your soul feels its disease indeed, you can surely find something to tell Christ.

Doubt not his willingness to save you, because you are a sinner. It is Christ's office to save sinners. He says himself, "I came not to call the righteous, but sinners to repentance." Luke 5: 32.

Wait not because you feel unworthy. Wait for nothing. Wait for nobody. Waiting comes from the devil. Just as you are, go to Christ. The worse you are, the more need you have to apply to him. You will never mend yourself by staying away.

Fear not because your prayer is stammering, your words feeble, and your language poor. Jesus can understand you. Just as a mother understands the first lispings of her infant, so does the blessed Saviour understand sinners. He can read a sigh, and see a meaning in a groan.

Despair not because you do not get an answer immediately. While you are speaking, Jesus is listening. If he delays an answer, it is only for wise reasons, and to try if you are in earnest. The answer will surely come. Though it tarry, wait for it. It will surely come.

Oh, reader, if you have any desire to be saved, remember the advice I have given you this day. Act upon it honestly and heartily, and you shall be saved.

3. Let me speak, lastly, TO THOSE WHO DO PRAY. I trust that some who read this tract know well what prayer is, and have the Spirit of adoption. To all such, I offer a few

26

words of brotherly counsel and exhortation. The incense offered in the tabernacle was ordered to be made in a particular way. Not every kind of incense would do. Let us remember this, and be careful about the matter and manner of our prayers.

Brethren who pray, if I know anything of a Christian's heart, you are often sick of your own prayers. Ton never enter into the apostle's words, "When I would do good, evil is present with me," so thoroughly as you sometimes do upon your knees. You can understand David's words, "I hate vain thoughts." You can sympathize with that poor converted Hottentot who was overheard praying, "Lord, deliver me from all my enemies, and above all, from that bad man – myself." There are few children of God who do not often find the season of prayer a season of conflict. The devil has special wrath against us when he sees us on our knees. Yet, I believe that prayers which cost us no trouble, should be regarded with great suspicion. I believe we are very poor judges of the goodness of our prayers, and that the prayer which pleases us least, often pleases God most. Suffer me then, as a companion in the Christian warfare, to offer you a few words of exhortation. One thing, at least, we all feel: we must pray. We cannot give it up. We must go on.

I commend then to your attention, the importance of *reverence and humility in prayer*. Let us never forget what we are, and what a solemn thing it is to speak with God. Let us beware of rushing into his presence with carelessness and levity. Let us say to ourselves: "I am on holy ground. This is no other than the gate of heaven. If I do not mean what I say, I am trifling with God. If I regard iniquity in my heart, the Lord will not hear me." Let us keep in mind the words of Solomon, "Be not rash with thy mouth, and let not thy heart be hasty to utter anything before God; for God is in heaven, and thou on earth." Eccl. 5:2. When Abraham spoke to God, he said, "I am dust and ashes." When Job spoke to God, he said, "I am vile." Let us do likewise.

I commend to you the importance of praying spiritually. I mean by that, that we should labor always to have the direct help of 4he Spirit in our prayers, and beware above all things of formality. There is nothing so spiritual but that it may become a form, and this is specially , true of private prayer. We may insensibly get into the habit of using the fittest possible words, and offering the most scriptural petitions, and yet do it all by rote without feeling it, and walk daily round an old beaten path. I desire to touch this point with caution and delicacy. I know that there are certain great things we daily want, and that there is nothing necessarily formal in asking for these things in the same words. The world, the devil, *and our hearts, are daily the same. Of necessity we must daily go over old ground. But this I say, we must be very careful on this point. If the skeleton and outline of our prayers be by habit almost a form, let us strive that the clothing and filling up of our prayers, be as far as possible of the Spirit. As to praying out of a book in our private devotions, it is a habit I cannot praise. If we can tell our doctors the state of our bodies without a book, we ought to be able to tell the state of our souls to God. I have no objection to a man using crutches

28

when he is first recovering from broken limb. It is better to use crutches, than not to walk at all. But if I saw him all his life on crutches, T should not think it matter for congratulation. I should like to see him strong enough to throw his crutches away.

I commend to you the importance of making prayer *a regular business of life.* I might say something of the value of regular times in the day for prayer. God is a God of order. The hours for morning and' evening sacrifice in the Jewish temple were not fixed as they were without a meaning. Disorder is eminently one of the fruits of sin. But I would not bring any under bondage. This only I say, that it is essential to your soul's health to make praying a part of the business of every twenty – four hours in your life. Just as you allot time to eating, sleeping, and business^ so also allot time to prayer. Choose your own hours and seasons. At the very least, speak with God in the morning, before you speak with the world: and speak with God at night after you have done with the world. But settle it in your minds, that prayer is one of the great things of every day. Do not drive it into a corner. Do not give it the scraps and parings of your duty. Whatever else you make a business of, make a business of prayer.

I commend to you the importance or perseverance in prayer. Once having begun the habit, never give it up. Your heart will sometimes say, "You have had family prayers: what mighty harm if you leave private prayer undone?" Your body will sometimes say, "You are unwell, or sleepy, or weary; you need not pray." Your mind will sometimes say, "You have important business to attend to today cut short your prayers." Look on all such suggestions as coming direct from Satan. They are all as good as saying, "Neglect your soul." I do not maintain that prayers should always be of the same length; but I do say, let no excuse make you give up prayer. Paul said, "Continue in prayer," and, "Pray without ceasing." He did not mean that men should be always on their knees, but he did mean that our prayers should be, like the continual burnt – offering, steadily persevered in every day; that it should be like seed – time and harvest, and summer and "winter, unceasingly coming round at regular seasons; that it should be like the fire on the altar, not always consuming sacrifices, but never completely going out. Never forget that you may tie together morning and evening devotions, by an endless chain of short ejaculatory prayers throughout the day. Even in company, or business, or in the very streets, you may be silently sending up little winged messengers to God, as Nehemiah did in the very presence of Artaxerxes. And never think that time is wasted which is given to God. A nation does not become poorer because it loses one year of working days in seven, by keeping the Sabbath. A Christian never finds he is a loser, in the long run, by persevering in prayer. '

I commend to you the importance of earnestness in prayer. It is not necessary that a man should shout, or scream, or be very loud, in order to prove that he' is in earnest. But it is desirably that we should be hearty and fervent and warm, and ask as if we were really interested in what we were doing. It is the "effectual fervent" prayer that "availeth much." This is the lesson that is taught us by the expressions used in Scripture about prayer. It is called, "crying, knocking, wrestling, laboring, striving." This is the lesson taught us by scripture examples. Jacob is one. _ He said to the angel at Penuel, "I will not let thee go, except thou bless me." Gen. 32: 26. Daniel is another. Hear how he pleaded with God: "0 Lord, hear; Lord, forgive; O Lord,, hearken and do; defer not, for thine own sake, O my God." Dan. 9: 19. Our Lord Jesus Christ is another. It is written of him, "In the days of his flesh, he offered up prayers and supplications with strong crying and tears." Heb. 5: 7. Alas, how unlike is this to _many of our supplications! How tame and lukewarm they seem by comparison. How truly might God say to many of us, "You do not really want what you pray for." Let us try to amend this fault. Let us knock loudly at the door of grace, like Mercy in "Pilgrim's Progress," as if we must perish unless heard. Let us settle it in our minds, that cold prayers are a sacrifice without fire. Let us remember the story of Demosthenes the great orator, when one came to him, and wanted him to plead his cause. He heard him without attention, while he told his story without earnestness. The man saw this, and cried out with anxiety that it was all true. "Ah," said Demosthenes, "1 believe you now."

I commend to you the importance of *praying with faith.* We should endeavor to believe that our prayers are heard, and that, if we ask things according to God's will, we shall be answered. This is the plain command of our Lord Jesus

Christ: "Whatsoever things ye desire, when ye pray, believe that ye receive them, and ye shall have them." Mark 11: 24. Faith is to prayer what the feather is to the arrow: without it prayer will not hit the mark. We should cultivate the habit of pleading promises in our prayers.

We should take with us some promise, and say, "Lord, here is thine own word pledged. Do for us as thou hast said." This was the habit of Jacob and Moses and David. The 119th Psalm is full of things asked, "according to thy word." Above all, we should cultivate the habit of expecting answers to our prayers. "We should do like the merchant who sends his ships to sea. We should not be satisfied, unless we see some return. Alas, there are few points on which Christians come short so much as this. , The church at Jerusalem made prayer without ceasing for Peter in prison; but when the prayer was answered, they would hardly believe it. Acts 12: 15. It is a solemn saying of Traill, "There is no surer mark of trifling in prayer, than when men are careless what they get by prayer."

I commend to you the importance of boldness in prayer. There is an unseemly familiarity in some men's prayers which I cannot praise. But there is such a thing as a holy boldness, which is exceedingly to be desired. I mean such boldness as that of Moses, when he pleads with God not to destroy Israel: "Wherefore," says he, "should the Egyptians speak and say, For mischief did he bring them out, to slay them in the mountains? Turn from thy fierce anger." Exod. 32: 12. I mean such boldness as that of Joshua, when the children of' Israel were defeated before men of Ai: "What," says he, "wilt thou do unto thy great name?" Josh. 7: 9. This is the boldness for which Luther was remarkable. One who heard him praying said, "What a spirit, what a confidence was in his very expressions. With such a reverence he sued, as one begging of God, and yet with such hope and assurance, as if he spoke with a loving father or friend." This is the boldness which distinguished Bruce, a great Scotch divine of the seventeenth century. His prayers were said to be "like bolts shot up into heaven." Here also I fear we sadly come short. We do not sufficiently realize the believer's privileges. We do not plead as often as we might, "Lord, are we not thine own people? Is it not for thy glory that we should be sanctified? Is it not for thy honor that thy gospel should increase?" '

I commend to you the importance of *fullness* in prayer. I do not forget that our Lord warns us against the example of the Pharisees, who, for pretence, made long prayers; and commands us when we pray not to use vain repetitions. But I cannot forget, on the other hand, that he has given his own sanction to large and long devotions by continuing all night in prayer to God. At all events, we are not likely in this day to err on the side of praying *too much*. Might it not rather be feared that many believers in this generation pray *too little*? Is not the actual amount o^ time that many Christians give to prayer, in the aggregate, very small? I am afraid these questions cannot be answered satisfactorily. I am afraid the private devotions of many are most painfully scanty and limited; just enough to prove they are alive and no more. They really seem to want little from God. They seem to have little to confess, little to ask for, and little to thank him for.

Alas, this is altogether wrong. Nothing is more common than to hear believers complaining that they do not get on. They tell us that they do not grow in grace as they could desire. Is it not rather to be suspected that many have quite as much grace as they ask for? Is it not the true account of many, that they have little, because they ask little? The cause of their weakness is to be found in their own stunted, dwarfish, climpped, contracted, hurried, narrow, diminutive prayers. They have not, because they ash not. Oh, we are not straitened in Christ, but in ourselves. The Lord says, "Open thy mouth wide, and I will fill it." But we are like the King of Israel who smote on the ground thrice and stayed, when he ought to have smitten five or six times.

I commend to you the importance of *particularity* in prayer. We ought not to be content with great general petitions. We ought to specify our wants before the throne of grace. It should not be enough to confess we are sinners; we should name the sins of which our conscience tells us we are most guilty. It should not be enough to ask for holiness; we should name the graces in which we feel most deficient. It should not be enough to tell the Lord we are in trouble; we should describe our trouble and all its peculiarities. This is what Jacob did when he – feared his brother Esau. He tells God exactly what it is that he fears. Gen. 32 :11. This is what Eliezer did, when he sought a wife for his master's son. He spreads before God precisely what he wants. Gen. 24:12. This is what Paul did when he had a thorn in the flesh. He besought the Lord. 2 Cor. 12:8. This is true faith and confidence. We should believe that nothing is too small to be named before God. What should we think of the patient who told his doctor he was ill, but never went into particulars? What should we think of the wife who told her husband she was unhappy, but did not specify the cause? What should we think of the child who told his father he was in trouble, but nothing more? Christ is the true bridegroom of the soul, the true physician of the heart, the real father of all his people. Let us show that we feel this by being unreserved in our communications with him. Let us hide no secrets from him. Let us tell him all our hearts.

I commend to you the importance of *intercession* in our prayers. We are all selfish by nature, and our selfishness is very apt to stick to us, even when we are converted. There is a tendency in us to think only of our own souls, our own spiritual conflicts, our own progress in religion, and to forget others. Against this tendency we all have need to watch and strive, and not least in our prayers. We should study to be of a public spirit. We should stir ourselves up to name other names besides our own before the throne of grace. We should try to bear in our hearts the whole world, the heathen, the Jews, the Roman – catholics, the body of true believers, the professing Protestant churches, the country in which we live, the congregation to which we belong, the household in – which we sojourn, the friends and relations we are connected with. For each and all of these we should plead. This is the highest charity. He loves me best who loves me in his prayers. This is for our soul's health. It enlarges our sympathies and expands our hearts. This is for the benefit of the church. The wheels of all machinery for extending the gospel are moved by prayer. They do as much for the Lord's cause who intercede like Moses on the mount, as they do who fight like Joshua in the thick of the battle. This is to be like Christ. He bears the names of his people, as their High Priest, before the Father. Oh, the privilege of being like Jesus ! This is to be a true helper to ministers. If I must choose a congregation, give me a people that pray.

I commend to you the importance of *thankfulness* in prayer. I know well that asking God is one thing and praising God is another. But I see so close a connection between prayer and praise in the Bible, that I dare not call that true prayer in which says, "By prayer and supplication, with thanksgiving, let your requests be made known unto God." Phil. 4: 6. "Continue in prayer, and watch in the same with thanksgiving." Colos. 4:2. It is of mercy that we are not in hell. It is of mercy that we have the hope of heaven. It is of mercy that we live in a land of spiritual light. It is of mercy that we have been called by the Spirit, and not left to reap the fruit of our own ways. It is of mercy that we still live and have opportunities of glorifying God actively or passively. Surely these thoughts should crowd on our minds whenever we speak with God. Surely we should never open our lips in prayer without blessing God for that free grace by which we live, and for that loving kindness which endureth for ever. Never was there an eminent saint who was not full of thankfulness. St. Paul hardly ever writes an epistle without beginning with thankfulness. Men like Whitefield in the last century, and Bickersteth in our time, abounded in thankfulness. Oh, reader, if we would be bright and shining lights in our day, we must cherish a spirit of praise. Let our prayers be thankful prayers. "

I commend to you the importance of watchfulness over your prayers. Prayer is that point in religion at which you must be most of all on your guard. Here it is that true religion begins; here it flourishes, and here it decays. Tell me what a man's prayers are, dnd I will soon tell you the state of his soul. Prayer is the spiritual pulse. By this the spiritual health may be tested. Prayer is the spiritual weather – glass. By this we may know whether it is fair or foul with our hearts. Oh, let us keep an eye continually upon our private devotions. Here is the pith and marrow of our practical Christianity. Sermons and books and tracts, and committee – meetings and the company of good men, are all good in their way, but they will never make up for the neglect of private prayer. Mark well the places and society and companions that unhinge your hearts for communion with God and make your prayers drive heavily. *There be on your guard.* Observe narrowly what friends and what employments leave your soul in the most spiritual frame, and most ready to speak with God. *To these cleave and stick fast.* If you will take care of your prayers, nothing shall go very wrong with your soul. '

I offer these points for your private consideration. I do it in all humility. I know no one who needs to be reminded of them more than I do myself. But I believe them to be God's own truth, and I desire myself and all I love to feel them more.

I want the times we live in to be praying times. I want the Christians of our day to be praying Christians. I want the church to be a praying church. My heart's desire and prayer in sending forth this tract is to promote a spirit of prayerfulness. I want those who never prayed yet, to arise and call upon God, and I want those who do pray, to see that they are not praying amiss.

HOW READEST THOU?

"What is written in the law? How readest thou?"

Luke X. 26.

Reader,

The question before your eyes is 1800 years old. It was asked by our Lord Jesus Christ. It was asked concerning the Bible. I invite you to consider this question. I warn you, it is just as mighty and important now as it was on the day when it came from our Lord's lips. I want to apply it to the conscience of every one who reads this tract, and to knock at the door of his heart. I would fain sound a trumpet in the ear of every one who speaks English, and cry aloud, "How readest thou? Dost thou read the Bible?" Why do I hold this question to be of such mighty importance? Why do I press it on the notice of every man, as a matter of life and death? Give me your attention for a few minutes, and you shall see. Follow me through the pages of this tract, and you shall hear why I ask, "HOW READEST THOU? – DOST THOU READ THE BIBLE? "

I. I ask, first of all, because there is no knowledge absolutely needful to a man's salvation, except a knowledge of the things which are to be found in the Bible.

We live in days when the words of Daniel are fulfilled before our eyes: – " Many run to and fro, and knowledge is increased." Schools are multiplying on every side. New colleges are set up. Old universities are reformed and improved. New books are continually coming forth. More is being taught, – more is being learned, – more is being read, than there ever was since the world began. It is all well. I Tejoice at it. An ignorant population is a perilous and expensive burden to any nation. It is a ready prey to the first Absalom, or Cataline, or Wat Tyler, or Jack Cade, who may arise to entice it to do evil. But this I say, – we must never forget, that all the education a man's head can receive, will not save his soul from hell, unless he knows the truths of the Bible.

A man *may have prodigious learning, and yet never be saved.* He may be master of half the languages spoken round the globe. He may be acquainted with the highest and deepest things in heaven and earth. He may have read books till he is like a walking encyclopedia. He may be familiar with the stars of heaven, – the birds of the air, – the beasts of the earth, and the fishes of the sea. He may be able to speak of plants, from the cedar of Lebanon to the hyssop that grows on the wall. He may be able to discourse of all the secrets of fire, air, earth, and water. And yet, if he dies ignorant of Bible truths, he dies a miserable man.

Chemistry never silenced a guilty conscience. Mathematics never healed a broken heart. All the sciences in the world never smoothed down a dying pillow. No earthly philosophy ever supplied hope in death. No natural theology ever gave peace in the prospect of meeting a holy God. All these things are of the earth, earthy, and can never raise a man above the earth's level. They may enable a man to strut and fret his little season here below with a more dignified gait than his fellow – mortals, but they can never give him wings, and enable him to soar towards heaven. He that has the largest share of them, will find at length that without Bible knowledge he has got no lasting possession. Death will make an end of all his attainments, and after death they will do him no good at all.

A man *may be a very ignorant man, and yet be saved.* He may be unable to read a word, or write a letter. He may know nothing of geography beyond the bounds of his own parish, and be utterly unable to say which is nearest, Paris or New York. He may know nothing of arithmetic, and not see any difference between a million and a thousand. He may know nothing of history, not even of his own land, and be quite ignorant whether his country owes most to Semiramis, Boadicea, or Queen Elizabeth. He may know nothing of the affairs of his own times, and be incapable of telling you whether the Chancellor of the Exchequer, or the Commander – in – Chief, or the Archbishop of Canterbury is managing the national finances. He may know nothing of science, and its discoveries, – and whether Julius Caesar won his victories with gunpowder, or the apostles had a printing press, or the sun goes round the earth, may be matters about which he has not an idea. And yet if that very man has heard Bible truth with his ears, and believed it with his heart, he knows enough to save his soul. He will be found at last with Lazarus in Abraham's bosom, while his scientific fellow – creature, who has died unconverted, is lost forever.

Knowledge of the Bible, in short, is the one knowledge that is needful. A man may get to heaven without money, learning, health, or friends, – but without Bible knowledge he will never get there at all. A man may have the mightiest of minds, and a memory stored with all that a mighty mind can grasp, – and yet, if he does not know the things of the Bible, he will make shipwreck of his soul forever. Woe! woe! woe to the man who dies in ignorance of the Bible!

Reader, this is the book about which I am addressing you to – day. It is no light matter what you do with such a book. It concerns the life of your soul. I summon you, I charge you to give an honest answer to my question. What are you doing with the Bible? – Do you read it? – HOW READEST THOU?

II. I ask, in the second place, because there is no book in existence written in such a manner as the Bible.

The Bible is "written by inspiration of God." In this respect it is utterly unlike all other writings. God taught the writers of it what to say. God put into their mind thoughts and ideas. God guided their pens in setting down those thoughts and ideas. When you read it, you are not reading the self – taught compositions of poor imperfect men like yourself, but the words of the eternal God. When you hear it, you are not listening to the erring opinions of short –

42

lived mortals, but to the unchanging mind of the King of kings. The men who were employed to indite the Bible, spoke not of themselves. They "spake as they were moved by the Holy Ghost." (2 Pet. i. 21).

I shall not waste time by attempting any long and labored proof of this. I say boldly, that the book itself is the best witness of its own inspiration. It is utterly inexplicable and unaccountable in any other point of view. It is the greatest standing miracle in the world. He that dares to say the Bible is not inspired, let him give a reasonable account of it, if he can. Let him explain the history and character of the book in a way that will satisfy any man of common sense. The burden of proof seems to my mind, to lie on him.

Here is a book, written by not less than fifty different persons. The writers were men of every rank and class in society. One was a lawgiver. One was a warlike king. One was a peaceful king. One was a herdsman. One had been brought up as a publican, – another as a physician, – another as a learned Pharisee, – two as fishermen, – several as priests. They lived at different intervals, over a space of 1500 years; and the greater part of them never saw each other face to face. And yet there is a perfect harmony among all these writers. They all write as if they were under one dictation. The handwriting may vary, but the mind that runs through their work is always one and the same. They all tell the same story. They all give one account of man, – one account of God, – one account of the way of salvation, – one account of the heart. You see truth unfolding under their hands, as you go through the volume of their writings, – but you never detect any real contradiction, or contrariety of view. Tell us not that all this might be the result of chance. The man who can believe that, must indeed be a credulous person. There is only one satisfactory account of the book. It was written under the direct inspiration of God.

Here is a book that has been finished and before the world for nearly 1800 years. These 1800 years have been the busiest and most changeful period the world has ever seen. During this period the greatest discoveries have been made in science, – the greatest alterations in the ways and customs of society, – the greatest improvements in the habits and usages of life. Hundreds of things might be named which satisfied and pleased our forefathers, which we have laid aside long ago as obsolete, useless, and old – fashioned. The laws, the books, the houses, the furniture, the clothes, the carriages of each succeeding century, have been a continual improvement on those of the century that went before. There is hardly a thing in which faults and weak points have not been discovered.

There is hardly an institution which has not gone through a process of sifting, purifying, refining, simplifying, reforming, amending, and changing. But all this time men have never discovered a weak point or defect in the Bible. Infidels have assailed it in vain. There it stands, – perfect, and fresh, and complete, as it did eighteen centuries ago. The march of intellect never overtakes it. The wisdom of wise men never gets beyond it. The science of philosophers never proves it wrong. The discoveries of travelers never convict it of mistakes. Are the distant islands of the Pacific laid open? – Nothing is found that in the slightest degree contradicts the Bible account of man's heart. Are the ruins of Nineveh and Egypt ransacked and explored? – Nothing is found that overturns one jot or tittle of the Bible's historical statements. Are the heathen in the remotest parts of the earth induced to give up their idols? – The Bible is found to meet the wants of their consciences, as thoroughly as it did those of Greeks and Romans in the days when it was first completed. It suits all ages, ranks, climates, minds, conditions. It is the one book which suits the world. How shall we account for this? What satisfactory explanation can we give? There is only one account and one explanation.

The Bible was written by inspiration. It is the book of the world, because He inspired it who formed the world, – who made all nations of one blood, – and knows man's common nature. It is the book for every heart, because He dictated it, who alone knows all hearts and what all hearts require. It is the book of God.

Here is a book, which for sublimity, wisdom, and purity, is utterly unrivaled. No other book in existence comes near it. There is a style and tone of thought about it, which separates it from all other writings. There are no weak points, and motes, and flaws, and blemishes. There is no mixture of infirmity and feebleness, such as you will find in the works of even the best Christians. "Holy, holy, holy," seems written on every page.

To talk of comparing the Bible with the Koran, the Shasters, or the book of Mormon, is positively absurd. You might as well compare the sun with a rushlight, – or Mount

Blanc with a mole hill, – or St. Paul's with an Irish hovel, – or the Portland vase with a garden pot, – or the Koh – i – noor diamond with a bit of glass. God seems to have allowed the existence of these pretended revelations, in order to prove the immeasurable superiority of His own word. To talk of the inspiration of the Bible, as only differing in degree from that of such writings as the works of Emerson, Gibbon, and Voltaire, is simply a piece of blasphemous folly. Every honest and unprejudiced reader must see that there is a gulf between the Bible, and any other book, which no man can fathom. You feel at turning from the Scriptures to other works, that you have got into a new atmosphere. You feel like one who has exchanged gold for base metal, and heaven for earth. And how can this mighty difference be accounted for? The men who wrote the Bible had no special advantages. They had, most of them, little leisure, few books, and no learning, – such as learning is reckoned in this world. Yet the book they compose is one which is unrivaled! There is but one way of accounting for this. They wrote under the direct inspiration of God.

It proves nothing, against inspiration, as some have asserted, that the writers of the Bible have each a different style. Isaiah does not write like Jeremiah, and Paul does not write like John. This is perfectly true – and yet the works of these men are not a whit less equally inspired. The waters of the sea have many different shades. In one place they look blue, and in another green. And yet the difference is owing to the depth or shallowness of the part we see, or to the nature of the bottom. The water in every case is the same salt sea. The breath of a man may produce different sounds, according to the character of the instrument on which he plays. The flute, the pipe, and the trumpet, have each their peculiar note. And yet the breath that calls forth the notes, is in each case one and the same. The light of the planets we seen in heaven, is very various. Mars, and Saturn, and Jupiter, have each a peculiar color. And yet we know that the light of the sun, which each planet reflects, is in each case one and the same.

Just in the same way, the books of the Old and New Testaments are all inspired truth, and yet the aspect of that truth varies according to the mind through which the Holy Ghost makes it flow. The hand – writing and style of the writers differ enough to prove that each had a distinct individual being; but the Divine Guide who dictates and directs the whole is always one. All is alike inspired. Every chapter, and verse, and word, is from God.

Oh! that men who are troubled with doubts, and questionings, and skeptical thoughts about inspiration, would calmly examine the Bible for themselves! Oh! that they would act on the advice which was the first step to Augustine's conversion, –

" Take it up and read it! – take it up and read it."

How many Gordian knots this course of action would cut! How many difficulties and objections would vanish away at once like mist before the rising sun! How many would soon confess, "The finger of God is here! God is in this book, and I knew it not."

Reader, this is the book about which I address you this

day. Surely it is no light matter what you are doing with this book. It is no light thing that God should have caused this book to be "written for your learning," and that you should have before you "the oracles of God." I charge you, I summon you to give an honest answer to my question. What art thou doing with the Bible? Dost thou read it at all? – HOW READEST THOU?

III. I ask, in the third place, because no book in existence contains such important matter as the Bible.

The Bible handles subjects which are utterly beyond the reach of man, when left to himself. It treats of things that are invisible, – the soul, – the world to come, – and eternity; – subjects which man has no line to fathom. All who have tried to write on these subjects, without Bible light, have done little but show their own ignorance. They grope like the blind. They speculate. They conjecture. They generally make the darkness more visible, and land us in a region of uncertainty and doubt. How little did the wisest of the heathen know! How dim were the views of Solon, Socrates, Aristotle, Plato, Cicero, and Seneca! A well – taught Sunday – school child, in the present day, knows more eternal truth than all these sages put together.

The Bible alone describes the beginning and end of the globe on which we live. It starts from the birth – day of the sun, moon, stars, and earth, and shows us creation in its cradle. It foretells minutely the dissolution of all things, – when the stars shall fall from their places, and the earth, and all its works, shall be burned up, – and shows us creation in its grave. It tells us the story of the world's youth, and it tells us the story of its old age. It gives us the picture of its first days, and it gives us the picture of its last. How vast and important is this knowledge!

The Bible alone gives a true and faithful account of man. It does not flatter him as novels and romances do. It does not conceal his faults and exaggerate his goodness. It paints him just as he is. It describes him as a fallen creature, very far gone from original righteousness, and of his own nature inclined to evil, – a creature needing not only a pardon, but a new heart, to make him fit for heaven. It shows him to be a corrupt being, under every possible circumstance, when left to himself; – corrupt after the loss of paradise, – corrupt after the flood, – corrupt when fenced in by laws and commandments, – corrupt when the Son of God visited him as manifest in the flesh, – corrupt in the face of warnings, – corrupt in the face of miracles, – corrupt in the face of judgments, – corrupt in the face of mercies. In one word, – it shows man to be by nature always a sinner. How important is this knowledge!

The Bible alone gives us true views of God. By nature man knows nothing of Him. All his conceptions and ideas of Him are low, groveling, and debased. What can be more degraded than the gods of the Canaanites, and Egyptians, – of Babylon, of Greece, and of Rome? What can be more vile than the gods of the Hindoos, and other heathens, in our own times? By the Bible we know that God hates sin. – The destruction of the world by the flood, – the burning of

Sodom and Gomorrah, – the drowning of Pharaoh and the Egyptians in the Red Sea, – the cutting off of the nations of Canaan, – the overthrow of Jerusalem and the temple, – the scattering of the Jews; – all these are unmistakable witnesses.

By the Bible we know that God loves sinners. His gracious promise in the day of Adam's fall, – His long suffering in the times of Noah, – His deliverance of Israel out of the land of Egypt, – His gift of the law at Mount Sinai, – His bringing the tribes into the promised land, – His forbearance in the days of the judges and kings, – His repeated warnings by the mouth of His prophets, – His restoration of Israel, after the Babylonian captivity, – His sending His Son into the world, in due time, to be crucified, – His commanding the Gospel to be preached to the Gentiles; – all these are speaking facts.

By the Bible we learn that God knows all things. We see Him foretelling things hundreds and thousands of years before they take place, and as he foretells so it comes to pass. He foretold that the family of Ham should be a servant of servants, – that Tyre should become a rock for drying nets, – that Nineveh should become a desolation, – that Babylon should be made a desert, – that Egypt should be the basest of kingdoms, – and that the Jews should not be reckoned among the nations. All these thing were utterly unlikely. Yet all have been fulfilled. Reader, once more I say, how important is this knowledge! The Bible alone teaches us that God has made a full, perfect, and complete provision for the salvation of fallen man. It tells us of an atonement made for the sin of the .world, by the sacrifice and death of God's own Son upon the cross. It tells us that by His death for sinners, He obtained eternal redemption for all that believe on Him. The claims of God's broken law have now been satisfied. Christ has suffered for sin, the just for the unjust. God can now be just, and yet the justifier of the ungodly. It tells us that there is now a complete remedy for the guilt of sin, – even the precious blood of Christ. Whosoever believeth on Him shall not perish, but have eternal life. It tells us that there is a complete remedy for the power of sin, – even the almighty grace of the Spirit of Christ. It shows us the Holy Ghost quickening believers, and making them new creatures. It promises a new heart and a new nature to all who will hear Christ's voice, and follow him. Reader, once more I say, how important is this knowledge!

The Bible alone explains the state of things that ice see in the world around us. There are many things on earth which a natural man cannot explain. The amazing inequality of conditions, – the poverty and distress, – the oppression and persecution, – the shakings and tumults, – the failures of statesmen and legislators, – the constant existence of uncured evils and abuses, – all these things are often puzzling to him. He sees, but does not understand. But the Bible makes it all clear. The Bible can tell him that the whole world lieth in wickedness, – that the prince of the world, the devil, is everywhere, and that it is vain to look for perfection in the present order of things. The Bible will tell him that neither laws nor education can ever change men's hearts, – and that just as no man will ever make a machine work well, unless he allows for friction, – so also no man will do much good in the world, unless he always remembers that the world he works in is full of sin. The Bible will tell him that there is "a good time" certainly coming, – and coming perhaps sooner than people expect it, – a time of perfect knowledge, perfect justice, perfect happiness, and perfect peace. But the Bible will tell him this time shall not be brought in by any power but that of Christ coming to earth again. And for that second coming of Christ the Bible will tell him to prepare. Oh! reader, how important is all this knowledge!

But time would fail me, if I were to enter fully into all the great things which the Bible reveals. It is not by any sketch or outline that the treasures of the Bible can be displayed. It would be easy to point out many other things, besides those I have mentioned, and yet the half of its riches would be left untold.

How comforting is the account it gives us of the great mediator of the New Testament, – the man Christ Jesus! Four times over His picture is graciously drawn before our eyes. Four separate witnesses tell us of His miracles and His ministry, – His sayings and His doings, – His life and His death, – His power and His love, – His kindness and His patience, – His ways, His words, His works, His thoughts, His heart. Blessed be God, there is one thing in the Bible, the most prejudiced reader can hardly fail to understand, and that is the character of Jesus Christ!

How encouraging are the examples the Bible gives us of good people! It tells us of many who were of like passions with ourselves, – men and women who had cares, crosses, families, temptations,, afflictions, diseases, like ourselves, – and yet by faith and patience inherited the promises, and got safe home. It keeps back nothing in the history of these people. Their mistakes, their infirmities, their conflicts, their experience, their prayers, their praises, their useful lives, their happy deaths, – all are fully recorded. And it tells us the God and Saviour of these men and women still waits to be gracious, and is altogether unchanged.

How instructive are the examples the Bible gives us of bad people! It tells us of men and women who had light, and knowledge, and opportunities, like ourselves, and yet hardened their hearts, loved the world, clung to their sins, would have their own way, despised reproof, and ruined their own souls forever. And it warns us that the God who punished Pharaoh, and Saul, and Ahab, and Jezebel, and Judas, and Ananias and Sapphira, is a God who never alters, and that there is a hell.

How precious are the promises which the Bible contains for the use of those who love God! There is hardly any possible emergency or condition for which it has not some word in season. And it tells men that God loves to be put in remembrance of these promises, and that if He has said He will do' a thing, His promise shall certainly be performed.

How blessed are the hopes which the Bible holds out to the believer in Christ Jesus! Peace in the hour of death, – rest and happiness on the other side of the grave, ^a glorious body in the morning of the resurrection, – a full and triumphant acquittal in the day of judgment, – an everlasting reward in the kingdom of Christ, – a joyful meeting with the Lord's people in the day of gathering together ; – these, these are the future prospects of every true Christian. They are all written in the book. – in the book which is all true.

How striking is the light which the Bible throws on the character of man! It teaches us what men may be expected to be, and do, in every position and station of life. It gives us the deepest insight into the secret springs and motives of human actions, and the ordinary course of events under the control of human agents. It is the true discerner of the thoughts and intents of the heart. How deep is the wisdom contained in the books of Proverbs and Ecclesiastes! I can well understand an old divine saying, "Give me a candle and a Bible, and shut me up in a dark dungeon, and I will tell you all that the whole world is doing."

Reader, all these are things which men could find nowhere except in the Bible. We have probably not the least idea how little we should know about these things if we had not the Bible. We hardly know the value of the air we breathe, and the sun which shines on us, because we have never known what it is to be without them. We do not value the truths on which I have been just now dwelling, because we do not realize the darkness of men to whom these truths have not been revealed. Surely no tongue can fully tell the value of the treasures this one volume contains. Well might old John Newton say that some books were copper books in his estimation, some were silver, and some few were gold; – but the Bible alone was like a book all made up of bank notes.

Think not for a moment that any part of this precious book is not profitable. Think not that such portions as catalogues and pedigrees, – as Leviticus, and the description of Ezekiel's temple, – are useless and without value. Believe me it is childish folly to question the usefulness of any word in the Bible merely because our eyes at present do not see its use.

Come with me and look for a moment at the book of nature, and I will soon show you things of which you do not see the use.

Place yourself in imagination by the side of an Australian gold – digging, and observe the earth that is drawn up from its bottom. It is likely that your unpractised eye will see nothing in that heap but rubbish, and dirt, and stones. And yet that very heap of earth may prove on washing to be full of particles of the purest gold. It is just the same with the Bible. "We see but a little of it now. We shall find hereafter that every word of it contained gold.

Place yourself in imagination on the top of some Highland mountain. Look at the minute moss or lichen which clings to the side of that mass of rock. Tell me if you can what use and purpose that lichen serves. The birds of the air, the beasts of the field, the very insects leave it alone. The grouse, and ptarmigan, and red deer draw no sustenance from it. The rock does not require its covering. And yet that minute lichen is as truly a part of God's creation as the cedars of Lebanon, or the Victoria Regia of the South American rivers. Place it under a microscope, and you will soon see that like all other works of God it is "very good," and full of beautiful design. Settle it down in your mind, that as it is with the book of nature, so it is with the book of Revelation, the written Word of God. There is not a chapter or verse from first to last, which is not in some way profitable. If you and I do not see its use, it is because we have not eyes to see it yet.

But all, we may rest assured, is precious. All is very good. Well said Bishop Jewell,

"There is no sentence, no clause, no word, no syllable, no letter, but it is written for thy instruction. There is not one jot, but it is signed and sealed with the blood of the Lamb."

Reader, this is the book about which I address you this day. Surely it is no light matter what you are doing with it. It is no light matter in what way you are using this treasure. I charge you, I summon you to give an honest answer to my question, – What art thou doing with the Bible? – Dost thou read it? – HOW READEST THOU?

IV. I ask in the fourth place, because no book in existence has produced such wonderful effects on mankind at large as the Bible.

This is the book whose doctrines turned the world upside down in the days of the apostles.

Eighteen centuries have now passed away since God sent forth a few Jews from a remote corner of the earth to do a work which according to man's judgment must have seemed impossible. He sent them forth at a time when the whole world was full of superstition, cruelty, lust, and sin.

He sent them forth to proclaim that the established religions of the earth were false and useless, and must be forsaken. He sent them forth to persuade men to give up old habits and customs, and to live different lives. He sent them forth to do battle with vested interests, with old associations, with a bigoted priesthood, with sneering philosophers, with an ignorant population, with bloody – minded emperors, with the whole influence of Eome. Never was there an enterprise to all appearance more Quixotic, and less likely to succeed!

And how did He arm them for this battle? He gave them no carnal weapons. He gave them no worldly power to compel assent, and no worldly riches to bribe belief. He simply put the Holy Ghost into their hearts, and the Scriptures into their hands. He simply bade them to expound and explain, to enforce and to publish the doctrines of the Bible. The preacher of Christianity in the first century was not a man with a sword and an army, to frighten people, like Mahomet, – or a man with a license to be sensual, to allure people, like the priests of the shameful idols of Hindostan. No! he was nothing more than one holy man with one holy book.

And how did these men of one book prosper? In a few generations they entirely changed the face of society by the doctrines of the Bible. They emptied the temples of the heathen gods. They famished idolatry, or left it high and dry like a stranded ship. They brought into the world a higher tone of morality between man and man. They raised the character and position of woman. They altered the standard of purity and decency. They put an end to many cruel and bloody customs, such as the gladiatorial fights. There was no stopping the change. Persecution and opposition were useless. One victory after another was won. One bad thing after another melted away. Whether men liked it or not, they were insensibly affected by the movement of the new religion, and drawn within the whirlpool of its power. The earth shook, and their rotten refuges fell to the ground. The flood rose, and they found themselves obliged to rise with it. The tree of Christianity swelled and grew, and the chains they had cast round it to arrest its growth, snapped like tow. And all this was done by the doctrines of the Bible! Talk of victories indeed! What are the victories of Alexander, and Caesar, and Marlborough, and Napoleon, and Wellington, compared with those I have just mentioned? For extent, for completeness, for results, for permanence, there are no victories like the victories of the Bible.

This is the book which turned Europe upside down in the days of the Protestant Reformation.

No man can read the history of Christendom as it was five hundred years age, and not see that darkness covered the whole professing church of Christ, even a darkness that might be felt. So great was the change that had come over Christianity, that if an apostle had risen from the dead he would not have recognized it, and would have thought that heathenism had revived again. The doctrines of the Gospel lay buried under a dense mass of human traditions. Penances, and pilgrimages, and indulgences, relic – worship, and, image – worship, and saint – worship, and worship of the Virgin Mary, formed the sum and substance of most people's religion. The church was made an idol. The priests and ministers of the church usurped the place of Christ. And by what means was all this miserable darkness cleared away? By none so much as by bringing forth once more the Bible. It was not merely the preaching of Luther and his friends, which established Protestantism in Germany. The grand lever which overthrew the Pope's power in that country, was Luther's translation of the Bible into the German tongue.

It was not merely the writings of Cranmer and the English Reformers which cast down popery in England. The seeds of the work thus carried forward were first sown by Wycliffe's translation of the Bible many years before. It was not merely the quarrel of Henry VIII and the Pope of Rome, which loosened the Pope's hold on English minds. It was the royal permission to have the Bible translated and set up in churches, so that every one who liked might read it. Yes! it was the reading and circulation of Scripture which mainly established the cause of Protestantism in England, in Germany, and Switzerland. Without it the people would probably have returned to their former bondage when the first reformers died. But by reading of the Bible the public mind became gradually leavened with the principles of true religion. Men's eyes became thoroughly open. Their spiritual understandings became thoroughly enlarged. The abominations of popery became distinctly visible. The excellence of the pure Gospel became a rooted idea in their hearts. It was then in vain for Popes to thunder forth excommunications. It was useless for kings and queens to attempt to stop the course of Protestantism by fire and sword. It was all too late. The people knew too much. They had seen the light. They had heard the joyful sound. They had tasted the truth. The sun had risen on their minds. The scales had fallen from their eyes. The Bible had done its appointed work within them, and that work was not to be overthrown. The people would not return to Egypt. The clock could not be put back again. A mental and moral revolution had been effected, and mainly effected by God's Word.

Oh! reader, those are the true revolutions which the Bible effects. "What are all the revolutions recorded by Vertot; what are all the revolutions which France and England have gone through, compared to these? No revolutions are so bloodless, none so satisfactory, none so rich in lasting results, as the revolutions accomplished by the Bible! This is the book on which the well – being of nations has always hinged, and with which the interests of every nation in Christendom at this moment are inseparably bound up. Just in proportion as the Bible is honored or not, light or darkness, morality or immorality, true religion or superstition, liberty or despotism, good laws or bad, will be found in a land. Come with me and open the pages of history, and you will read the proofs in time past. Read it in the history of Israel under the kings. How great was the wickedness that then prevailed! But who can wonder? The law of the Lord had been completely lost sight of, and was found in the days of Josiah in a corner of the temple. – Read it in the history of the Jews in our Lord Jesus Christ's time.

How awful the picture of Scribes and Pharisees, and their religion! But who can wonder? The Scripture was made void by man's traditions. – Read it in the history of the church of Christ in the middle ages. What can be worse than the accounts we have of ignorance and superstition? But who can wonder? The times might well be dark, when men had not the light of the Bible.

Come with me next and look at the map of the world, and see what a tale it tells! Which are the countries where the greatest amount of ignorance, superstition, immorality, and tyranny is to be found at this very moment? The countries in which the Bible is a forbidden or neglected book, – such countries as Italy, and Spain, and the South American States. Which are the countries where liberty, and public and private morality have attained the highest pitch? The countries where the Bible is free to all, like England, Scotland, and the United States.

Yes! when you know how a nation deals with the Bible, you may generally know what a nation is. Oh! that the rulers of some nations did but know that a free Bible is the grand secret of national prosperity, and that the surest way to make subjects orderly and obedient, is to allow a free passage to the living waters of God's Word! Oh! that the people of some countries did but see that a free Bible is the beginning of all real freedom, and that the first liberty they should seek after, is liberty for the apostles and prophets, – liberty to have a Bible in every house, and a Bible in every hand! Well said Bishop Hooper, "God in heaven and the king on earth have no greater friend than the Bible." It is a striking fact, that when British Sovereigns are crowned, they are publicly presented with the Bible, and told, "This book is the most valuable thing this world affords."

This is the book which at this moment is producing the mightiest moral and spiritual effects throughout the world. This is the secret of the wonderful success which attends the London City Mission, and the Irish Church Missions. This is the true account of that amazing move toward Protestantism which has lately taken place in several departments of France. Which are the cities of the earth where the fewest soldiers and police are required to keep order? – London, Manchester, Liverpool, New York, – cities which are deluged with Bibles. Which are the churches on earth which are producing the greatest effect on mankind? The churches in which the Bible is exalted. Which are the parishes in England and Scotland where religion and morality have the strongest hold? The parishes in which the Bible is most circulated and read. Who are the ministers in England who have the most real influence over the minds of the people? Not those who are ever crying "Church! Church!" but those who are faithfully preaching the Word.

Ah! reader, a church which does not honor the Bible, is as useless as a body without life, or a steam engine without fire. A minister who does not honor the Bible, is as useless as a soldier without arms, a builder without tools, a pilot without compass, or a messenger without tidings. It is cheap and easy work for Roman Catholics, Neologians, and friends of secular education, to sneer at those who love the Bible. But the Romanist, the Neologian, and the friends of mere secular education, have never yet shown us one New Zealand, one Tinnevelly, one Sierra Leone as the fruit of their principles. We only can do that who honor the Bible, and we say these are the works of the Word, and the proofs of its power.

This is the book to which the civilized world is indebted for many of its best and most praise – worthy institutions. Few probably are aware how many are the good things that men have adopted for the public benefit, of which the origin may be clearly traced up to the Bible. It has left lasting marks wherever it has been received. From the Bible are drawn many of the best laws by which society is kept in order. From the Bible has been obtained the standard of morality about truth, honesty, and the relations of man and wife, which prevails among Christian nations, and which, – however feebly respected in many cases, – makes so great a difference between Christians and heathens.

To the Bible we are indebted for that most merciful provision for the poor man, the Sabbath day. To the influence of the Bible we owe nearly every humane and charitable institution in existence. The sick, the poor, the aged, the orphan, the lunatic, the idiot, the blind, were seldom or never thought of before the Bible leavened the world. You may search in vain for any record of institutions for their aid in the histories of Athens or of Rome.

Ah! reader, many sneer at the Bible, and say the world would get on well enough without it, who little think how great are their own obligations to the Bible. Little does the infidel think as he lies sick in some of our great hospitals, that he owes all his present comforts to the very book he affects to despise. Had it not been for the Bible, he might have died in misery, uncared for, unnoticed, and alone. Verily the world we live in is fearfully unconscious of its debts. The last day alone, I believe, will tell the full amount of benefit conferred upon it by the Bible.

Reader, this wonderful book is the subject about which I address you this day. Surely it is no light matter what you are doing with the Bible. The swords of conquering generals, – the ship in which Nelson led the fleets of England to victory, – the hydraulic press which raised the tubular bridge at the Menai; – each and all of these are objects of interest as instruments of mighty power.

The book I speak of this day is an instrument a thousand – fold mightier still. Surely it is no light matter whether you are paying it the attention it deserves. I charge you, I summon you to give me an honest answer this day, – What art thou doing with the Bible? – Dost thou read it? HOW READEST THOU?

V. I ask in the fifth place, because no book in existence can do so much for every one who reads it rightly, as the Bible.

The Bible does not profess to teach the wisdom of this world. It was not written to explain geology or astronomy. It will neither instruct you in mathematics, nor in natural philosophy. It will not make you a doctor, or a lawyer, or an engineer.

But there is another world to be thought of, beside that world in which man now lives. There are other ends for which man was created, beside making money and working. There are other interests which he is meant to attend to, beside those of his body ; and those interests are the interests of his soul. It is the interests of the immortal soul which the Bible is especially able to promote. If you would know law, you may study Blackstone or Sugden. If you would know astronomy or geology, you may study Herschel and Buckland. But if you would know how to have your soul saved, you must study the written Word of God.

Reader, the Bible is "able to make a man wise unto salvation, through faith which is in Christ Jesus." It can show you the way which leads to heaven. It can teach you everything you need to know, point out everything you need to believe, and explain everything you need to do. It can show you what you are, – a sinner. It can show you what God is, – perfectly holy. It can show you the great giver of pardon, peace, and grace, – Jesus Christ. I have read of an Englishman who visited Scotland in the days of Blair, Rutherford, and Dickson, three famous preachers, – and heard all three in succession. He said that the first showed him the majesty of God, – the second showed him the beauty of Christ, – and the third showed him all his heart. It is the glory and beauty of the Bible, that it is always teaching these three things more or less, from the first chapter of it to the last.

The Bible, applied to the heart by the Holy Ghost, is the grand instrument by which souls are first converted to God.

That mighty change is generally begun by some text or doctrine of the Word, brought home to a man's conscience. In this way the Bible has worked moral miracles by thousands. It has made drunkards become sober, – unchaste people become pure, – thieves become honest, – and violent – tempered people become meek. It has wholly altered the course of men's lives. It has caused their old things to pass away, and made all their ways new. It has taught worldly people to seek first the kingdom of God. It has taught lovers of pleasure to become lovers of God. It has taught the stream of men's affections to run upwards instead of running downwards. It has made men think of heaven, instead of always thinking of earth, and life by faith, instead of living by sight. All this it has done in every part of the world. All this it is doing still. What are the Romish miracles which weak men believe, compared to all this, even if they were true? Those are the truly great miracles which are yearly worked by the Word.

The Bible, applied to the heart by the Holy Ghost, is the chief means by which men are built up and established in the faith, after their conversion. It is able to cleanse them, to sanctify them, to instruct them in righteousness, and to furnish them thoroughly for all good works. The Spirit ordinarily does these things by the written Word; sometimes by the Word read, and sometimes by the Word preached, but seldom, if ever, without the Word. The Bible can show a believer how to walk in this world so as to please God. It can teach him how to glorify Christ in all the relations of life, and can make him a good master, servant, subject, husband, father, or son. It can enable him to bear afflictions and privations without murmuring, and say, "It is well." It can enable him to look down into the grave, and say, "I fear no evil." It can enable him to think on judgment and eternity, and not feel afraid. It can enable him to bear persecution without flinching, and to give up liberty and life rather than deny Christ's truth. Is he drowsy in soul? – . It can awaken him. Is he mourning? – It can comfort him. Is he erring? – It can restore him. Is he weak? – It can make him strong. Is he in company? – It can keep him from evil. Is he alone? – It can talk with him. All this the Bible can do for all believers, – for the least as well as the greatest, – for the richest as well as the poorest. It has done it for thousands already, and is doing it for thousands every day.

Reader, the man who has the Bible, has everything which is absolutely needful to make him spiritually wise. He needs no priest to break the bread of life for him. He needs no ancient traditions, no writing of the fathers, no voice of the church, to guide him into all truth. He has the well of truth open before him, and what can he want more? Yes! though he be shut up alone in a prison, or cast on a desert island, – though he never see a church, or minister, or sacrament again, – if he has but the Bible, he has got the infallible guide, and wants no other. If he has but the will to read that Bible rightly, it shall certainly teach him the road that leads to heaven. It is here alone that infallibility resides. It is not in the church. It is not in the councils. It is not in ministers. It is only in the written Word.

I know well that many say that they have found no

saving power in the Bible. They tell us they have tried to read it, and have learned nothing from it. They can see in it nothing but hard and deep things. They ask us what we mean by talking of its power.

I answer that the Bible no doubt contains hard things, or else it would not be the book of God. It contains things hard to comprehend, but only hard because we have not grasp of mind to comprehend them. It contains things above our reasoning powers, but nothing that might not be explained, if the eyes of our understanding were not feeble and dim. But is not an acknowledgment of our own ignorance the very corner – stone and foundation of all knowledge? Must not many things be taken for granted in the beginning of every science, before we can proceed one step towards acquaintance with it? Do we not require our children to learn many things of which they cannot see the meaning at first? And ought we not then to expect to find deep things when we begin studying the Word of God, and yet to believe that if we persevere in reading it, the meaning of many of them will one day be made clear? No doubt we ought so to expect, and so to believe. We must read with humility. We must take much on trust. We must believe that what we know not now, we shall know hereafter, some part in this world, and all in the world to come.

But I ask that man who has given up reading the Bible, because it contains hard things, whether he did not find many things in it easy and plain? I put it to his conscience, whether he did not see great landmarks and principles in it all the way through? I ask him whether the things needful to salvation did not stand out boldly before his eyes, like the light – houses on English headlands from the Land's – end to the mouth of the Thames. What should we think of the captain of a steamer, who brought up at night in the entrance of the Channel, on the plea that he did not know every parish, and village, and creek, along the British coast? Should we not think him a lazy coward, when the lights on the Lizard, the Eddystone, and the Stark, and Portland, and St. Catherine's, and Beachy Head, and Dungeness, and the Forelands, were shining forth like so many lamps, to guide him up to the river? Should we not say, why did you not steer by the great leading lights? And what ought we to say to the man who gives up reading the Bible, because it contains hard things, when his own state, and the path to heaven, and the way to serve God, are all written down clearly and unmistakably, as with a sunbeam? Surely we ought to tell that man, that his objections are no better than lazy excuses, and do not deserve to be heard.

I know well that many raise the objection, that thousands read the Bible, and are not a whit the better for their reading. And they ask us, when this is the case, what becomes of the Bible's boasted power?

I answer, that the reason why so many read the Bible without benefit is plain and simple, – they do not read it in the right way. There is generally a right way and a wrong way of doing everything in the world; and just as it is with other things, so it is in the matter of reading the Bible. The Bible is not so entirely different from all other Books, as to make it of no importance in what spirit and manner you read it. It does not do good, as a matter of course, by merely running our eyes over the print, any more than the sacraments do good by mere virtue of our receiving them. It does not ordinarily do good, unless it is read with humility and earnest prayer. The best steam – engine that was ever built, is useless if a man does not know how to work it. The best sun – dial that was ever constructed, will not tell its owner the time of day, if he. is so ignorant as to put it up in the shade. Just as it is with that steam – engine, and that sun – dial, so it is with the Bible. When men read it without profit, the fault is not in the book, but in themselves.

I tell the man who doubts the power of the Bible, because many read it, and are no better for the reading,.that the abuse of a receipt for preserving the health of his body? What must be thought of you, if you despise the only sure receipt for the everlasting health of your soul? I charge you, I entreat you, to give an honest answer to my question. What dost thou do with the Bible? – Dost thou read it? – HOW READEST THOU?

VI. I ask in the sixth place, because no gift of God to man is so awfully neglected and misused as the Bible.

Man has an unhappy skill in abusing God's gifts. His privileges, and power, and faculties, are all ingeniously perverted to other ends than those for which they were bestowed. His speech, his imagination, his intellect, his strength, his time, his influence, his money, – instead of being used as instruments for glorifying his Maker, – are generally employed for his own selfish ends. And just as man naturally makes a bad use of his other mercies, so he does of the written word. One sweeping charge may be brought against the whole of Christendom, and that charge is neglect and abuse of the Bible.

Reader, I know that this charge sounds awful. Listen to me, and I will give you proofs to substantiate it. Awful as it – is, it is sadly true.

It is true of the Roman Catholic Church, from one end of the world to the other. For six hundred years that unhappy church has waged open war with the Bible, and has labored incessantly to prevent people reading it. By a rule deliberately passed in the great council of Trent, – by the bulls of Popes, – by the encyclical letters of Romish bishops, – by the repeated open hostility of Romish priests, – the views of the Church of Rome on this subject have been made fully manifest. Of all the numerous and soul – ruining errors of which the Church of Rome is guilty, none is more mischievous and productive of evil than its treatment of the Bible.

It is truly fearful to consider how thoroughly at variance God and the Church of Rome are about the Bible. The Lord God has declared positively, that Holy Scripture is "profitable," – that it is "given for our learning," – that it is "able to make men wise unto salvation," – that it is "the sword" which a soldier of Christ should be armed with, – that it is "a light for our feet," – and that all errors arise from ignorance of it. The Church of Rome, on the other hand, has declared positively, in the council of Trent, that "If the Holy

Scripture be everywhere allowed indiscriminately in the vulgar tongue, more harm than good will arise from it," – and that "If any one shall presume to read, or possess, a Bible, without a license, he shall not receive absolution, except he first deliver it up!" A license to read the Bible! What a blasphemous insult is this! It would sound as well to talk of a license to breathe God's air, or look at God's sun. Well may the Church of Rome be in gross darkness, when it pours such contempt on the written word.

It is useless to assert, as some do, that statements such as these are not correct. It is useless to tell us that Bibles are openly paraded for sale in Roman Catholic shop windows, in English towns. The Church of Borne dares not show itself yet in its true colors in England. It winks at practices contrary to its avowed principles, because it suits its purpose to do so. It throws dust in the eyes of simple people, by the appearance of toleration; and so blinds them to its real character. But the Church of Eorne at heart is always the same.

Ask any one who has lived in countries on the Continent, where the power of the Pope is unrestrained, and see what he will tell you. Ask any one, especially, who has lived in Italy, and been at Bome, and seen Roman Catholic religion in full bloom, and mark what kind of account he will give you. If a man would know what real, pure Presbyterianism is, he must go to Scotland. If he would know what real, pure Church – of – Englandism is, he must visit England. If he would know what real, pure, genuine Romanism is, he should go to Italy and Rome.

Is it not a fact, that to have or read an Italian Bible is one of the highest crimes an Italian can commit? He may commit adultery and fornication, – he may stab, or lie, or rob, or swear, or cheat, – and get absolution from his priest without much difficulty. But woe be to the Italian who dares to have or read God's holy word! That fact speaks volumes. Let that fact be thoroughly known all over the world.

Is it not a fact, that the Bible itself cannot be bought at Rome, unless with immense difficulty, and at an immense price? You may buy books of many other kinds and descriptions, – worthless French novels, – frivolous Italian poetry, – miserable lying accounts of pretended miracles, done by pretended saints, – prayers to the Virgin Mary, and all manner of literary rubbish. You may buy poisons, daggers, or intoxicating drinks. You may buy relics, and rosaries, and scapulars, and crucifixes. You may buy masses and services, and redeem your father's soul from purgatory. But one thing it is almost impossible to buy, and that is the one thing needful, – the written word of God. You may easily buy all means and appliances for doing the works of darkness. You cannot buy the grand help for doing the works of light, except at an enormous cost. That fact alone speaks volumes. Oh! that the world would awake, and know it! THE BIBLE IS PRACTICALLY A FORBIDDEN BOOK AT ROME.

Ah! reader, it is an awful thought, that all these insults to the Bible are perpetrated in the name of Christianity! It is an awful thought, that a day of reckoning is yet to come, and that God the Judge of all is just as jealous about His word, as about His name and day! It is an awful thought, that even the Emperor of China will rise up in judgment 'with the Pope, and condemn him; for he has lately decreed that the New Testament ia'a profitable book, and may be read! It is an awful thought, that this Bible – proscribing Church of Rome contains more members than any Church in the world! Surely I have a right to say, no gift of God is so neglected and misused as the Bible.

But the Church of Rome, unhappily, is not the only professedly Christian Church whose members are guilty in this matter. The charge of neglecting the Bible is one which may be brought home to the members of Protestant churches also, and among others to the Protestants of England and Scotland in the present day.

I write this statement down with sorrow. I dare say it will be received by some with surprise, if not with incredulity. But I write it down calmly and deliberately, and I am certain it is true.

I am well aware that there are more Bibles in Great Britain at this moment than there ever were since the world began. There is more Bible buying and Bible selling, – more Bible printing and Bible distributing, – than ever was since England was a nation. We see Bibles in every bookseller's shop, – Bibles of every size, price, and style, – Bibles great, and Bibles small, – Bibles for the rich, and Bibles for the poor. But all this time I fear we are in danger of forgetting, that to have the Bible is one thing, and to read it is quite another.

I am firmly persuaded that the Bible of many a man and

woman in Great Britain is never read at all. In one house it lies in a corner, stiff , cold, glossy, and fresh as it was when it came from the bookseller's shop. In another it lies on a table, with its owner's name written in it, – a silent witness against him day after day. In another it lies on some high shelf, neglected and dusty, to be brought down only on grand occasions, – such as a birth in the family, – like a heathen idol at its yearly festival. In another it lies deep down at the bottom of some box or drawer, – among the things not wanted, – and is never dragged forth into the light of day, until the arrival of sickness, the doctor, and death. Ah! these things are sad and solemn. But they are true.

I am firmly persuaded that many in Great Britain who read the Bible, do not read it aright. One man looks over a chapter on Sunday evening, – but that is all. Another reads a chapter every day to his servants at family prayers, – but that is all. A third goes a step further, and hastily reads a verse or two in private every morning, before he goes out of his house. A fourth goes further still, and reads as much as a chapter or two every day, though he does it in a great hurry, and omits it on the smallest pretext. But each and every one of these men does what he does in a heartless, scrambling, formal kind of way. He does it coldly as a duty. He does not do it with appetite and pleasure. He is glad when the task is over. He forgets it all when the book is shut. Oh! what a sad picture is this! But in multitudes of cases, oh! how true!

But how do I know all this? "What makes me speak so confidently? Listen to me a few moments, and I will lay before you some evidence. Neglect of the Bible is like disease of the body. It shows itself in the face of a man's conduct. It tells its own tale. It cannot be hid. I am sure that many neglect the Bible, because of the enormous ignorance of true religion which everywhere prevails. There are thousands of professing Christians in this Protestant country who know literally nothing about the Gospel. They could not give you the slightest account of its distinctive doctrines. They have no more idea of the meaning of conversion, grace, faith, justification, and sanctification, than of so many words and names in Arabic. If you were to ask them whether regeneration, and the new creature, were a beast, a man, or a doctrine, they could not tell. And can I suppose such persons read the Scriptures? I cannot suppose it. I do not believe they do.

I am sure that many neglect the Bible, because of the enormous ignorance of true religion which everywhere prevails. There are thousands of professing Christians in this Protestant country who know literally nothing about the Gospel. They could not give you the slightest account of its distinctive doctrines. They have no more idea of the meaning of conversion, grace, faith, justification, and sanctification, than of so many words and names in Arabic. If you were to ask them whether regeneration, and the new creature, were a beast, a man, or a doctrine, they could not tell. And can I suppose such persons read the Scriptures? I cannot suppose it. I do not believe they do.

I am sure that many neglect the Bible, because of the utter indifference with which they regard false doctrine. They will talk with perfect coolness of others having become Roman Catholics, or Socinians, or Mormons, as if it were all the same thing in the long run. And can I suppose such persons search the Scriptures? I cannot suppose it. I do not believe they do. I am sure that many neglect the Bible, because of the readiness with which they receive false doctrines. They are led astray by the first preacher of lies they meet with, who has a pleasant voice, a nice manner, and a gift of eloquent speech. They swallow all he says without enquiry, and believe him as implicitly as the Papists do the Pope. And can I suppose such persons search the Scriptures? I cannot suppose it. I do not believe they do.

I am sure that many neglect the Bible, because of the bitterness with which they contend for some little secondary unimportant point in religion. They make a "Shibboleth" of their own little cherished point, and are ready to set down every one as no Christian, if he does not see it with their eyes. And can I suppose such persons really search the whole Scriptures? I cannot suppose it. I do not believe they do.

I am sure that many neglect the Bible, because of the very scanty knowledge they have of its contents. They know a certain set of doctrines. They can repeat a certain string of hackneyed texts. But they never seem to get beyond this little string. Let a man talk to them about some text out of their beaten path, and he is at once out of their depth. They listen, but have nothing to say. Let a minister preach to them anything but the merest elements of Christianity, and they appear shocked at him as a rash and unsound teacher. In short, they seem content to remain in the condition described by St. Paul to the Hebrews, always unskilful in the word of righteousness, – always in a state of religious babyhood. And can I suppose such persons really search the Scriptures? I cannot suppose it. I do not believe they do.

I am sure that many neglect the Bible, because of the lives they live. They do the very things that God plainly forbids. They neglect the very things that God plainly commands. They break God's laws week after week without shame. And can I suppose such persons search the Scriptures? I allow that much knowledge of the Bible and much wickedness of heart may sometimes be found together. But when I see a wicked life, I generally believe there is a neglected Bible.

I am sure that many neglect the Bible, because of the deaths they die. They send for a minister in their last moments, and ask for the consolations of religion. And in what state are they found? They know nothing whatever of the way of salvation. They have to be told which are the first principles of the Gospel of Christ. And can I suppose such persons have searched the Scriptures? I cannot suppose it. I do not believe they have.

I bring forward all this evidence with sorrow. I know well it will be offensive to some. But I believe I have stated nothing but glaring facts, which every true Christian and true minister of Christ's Gospel will readily confirm. And I say that these facts prove the existence of a sore evil in Great Britain. – I mean a neglected Bible. These things would never be, if the Bible was thoroughly read by many, as well as possessed.

Ah! reader, it is a painful thought, that there should be so much profession of love to the Bible among us, and so little proof that the Bible is read! Here we are, as a nation, pluming ourselves on our Protestantism, and yet neglecting the foundation on which Protestantism is built! Here we are, thanking God with our lips, like the Pharisee, that we are not Papists, as some are, and yet dishonoring God's word! It is an awful thought, that the people of this country will be judged according to their light, and that so many of them should be keeping that light under a bushel! Truly I have cause for saying, no gift of God is so neglected as the Bible.

Reader, this neglected book is the subject about which I address you this day. Surely it is no light matter what you are doing with the Bible. Surely when the plague is abroad, you should search and see whether the plague – spot is on you. I charge you, I entreat you, to give an honest answer to my question. – "What art thou doing with the Bible? Dost thou read it? HOW READEST THOU?

VII. I ask in the seventh place, because the Bible is the only rule by which all questions of doctrine or of duty can be tried.

The Lord God knows the weakness and infirmity of our poor fallen understandings. He knows that, even after conversion, our perceptions of right and wrong are exceedingly indistinct. He knows how artfully Satan can gild error with an appearance of truth, and can dress up wrong with plausible arguments, till it looks like right.

Knowing all this, He has mercifully provided us with an unerring standard of truth and error, right and wrong, and has taken care to make that standard a written book, – even the Scripture.

No one can look round the world, and not see the wisdom of such a provision. No one, can live long, and not find out that he is constantly in need of a counsellor and adviser, – of a rule of faith and practice, on which he can depend. Unless he lives like a beast, without a soul and conscience, he will find himself constantly assailed by difficult and puzzling questions. He will be often asking himself, what must I believe? and what must I do?

The world is full of difficulties about points of doctrine. The house of error lies close alongside the house of truth. The door of one is so like the door of the other, that there is continual risk of mistakes.

Does a man read or travel much? He will soon find the most opposite opinions prevailing among those who are called Christians. He will discover that different persons give the most different answers to the important question, What shall I do to be saved? The Roman Catholic and the Protestant, – the Neologian and the Tractarian, – The Mormon and the Swedenborgian, – each and all will assert that he alone has the truth. Each and all will tell him that safety is to be found in his party. Each and all say, "Come with us." All this is puzzling. What shall a man do? Does he settle down quietly in some English or Scotch parish? He will soon find that even in our own land the most conflicting views are held. He will soon discover that there are serious differences among Christians, as to the comparative importance of the various parts and articles of the faith. One man thinks of nothing but Church government, – another of nothing but sacraments, services, and forms, – a third of nothing but preaching the Gospel. Does he' apply to ministers for a solution? He will perhaps find one minister teaching one doctrine, and another another. Does he go to the Bishops for help? He will find what one Bishop says is right, another says is wrong. All this is puzzling. What shall a man do?

There is only one answer to this question. A man must make the Bible alone his rule. He must receive nothing, and believe nothing, which is not according to the word. He must try all religious teaching by one simple test, – Does it square with the Bible? – What saith the Scripture? I would to God the eyes of the laity of this country were more open on this subject.

I would to God they would learn to weigh sermons, books, opinions, and ministers, in the scales of the Bible, and to value all according to their conformity to the word. I would to God they would see that it matters little who says a thing, – whether he be Father or Reformer, – Bishop or Archbishop, – Priest or Deacon, – Archdeacon or Dean. The only question is, – Is the thing said Scriptural? If it is, it ought to be received and believed. If it is not, it ought to be refused and cast aside. I fear the consequences of that servile acceptance of everything which the parson says, which is so common among many English laymen. I fear lest they be led they know not whither, like the blinded Syrians, and awake some day to find themselves in the power of Rome. Oh! that men in England would only remember for what the Bible was given them!

I tell English laymen that it is nonsense to say, as some do, that it is presumptuous to judge a minister's teaching by the word. When one doctrine is proclaimed in one parish, and another in another, people must read and judge for themselves. Both doctrines cannot be right, and both ought to be tried by the word. I charge them above all things, never to suppose that any true minister of the Gospel will dislike his people measuring all he teaches by the Bible. On the contrary, the more they read the Bible, and prove all he says by the Bible, the better he will be pleased. A false minister may say, "You have no right to use your private judgment: leave the Bible to us who are ordained." A true minister will say, "Search the Scriptures, and if I do not teach you what is Scriptural, do not believe me." A false minister may say, "Hear the Church," and "Hear me." A true minister will say, "Hear the word of God."

But the world is not only fall of difficulties about points of doctrine. It is equally full of difficulties about points of practice. Every professing Christian, who wishes to act conscientiously, must know that it is so. The most puzzling questions are continually arising.

He is tried on every side by doubts as to the line of duty, and can often hardly see what is the right thing to do is. He is tried by questions connected with the management of his worldly calling, if he is in business or in trade. He sometimes sees things going on of a very doubtful character,

– things that can hardly be called fair, straightforward, truthful, and doing as you would be done by. But then everybody in the trade does these things. They have always been done in the most respectable houses. There would be no carrying on a profitable business if they were not done. They are not things distinctly named and prohibited by God. All this is very puzzling. What is a man to do?

He is tried by questions of a political kind, if he occupies a high position in life. He finds that men do things in their public capacity, which they would not think of doing in their private one. He finds that men are expected to sacrifice their own judgment, private opinion, and conscience, to the interests of their own party, and to believe that the acts of their own political friends are always right, and the acts of their political opponents always wrong. All this is puzzling. What is a man to do?

He is tried by questions in the matter of speaking truth. He hears things said continually which he knows are not correct. He hears a false coloring put on stories, which he knows ought to wear a different aspect. He sees additions to, and subtractions from the whole truth. He sees evasions, and equivocations, and concealments of facts in every class of society, when self interests are at stake. He hears false compliments paid, and false excuses alleged, and false characters given. But then it is the way of the world. Everybody does so. Nobody means any harm by it. All this is very puzzling. What is he to do?

He is tried by questions about Sabbath observance. Can there really be any harm in traveling, or writing letters, or keeping accounts, or reading newspapers on Sunday? Is it wrong to take a situation on a railway, merely because the Sunday traffic would almost entirely keep him away from public worship? Would it be wrong to open the Crystal Palace at Sydenham on Sundays? Is not Christianity a religion of liberty? Do not many learned, and respectable, and titled people think that Sunday should be a day for recreation? All this is very puzzling. What is a man to do? He is tried by questions about worldly amusements. Races, and balls, and operas, and theatres, and card parties, are all very doubtful methods of spending time. But then he sees numbers of great people taking part in them. Are all these people wrong? Can there really be such mighty harm in these things? All this is very puzzling. What is a man to do?

He is tried by questions about the education of his children. He wishes to train them up morally and religiously, and to remember their souls. But he is told by many sensible people that young persons will be young, – that it does not do to check and restrain them too much, and that he ought to attend pantomimes and children's parties, and give children's balls himself. He is informed that this nobleman or that lady of rank, always does so, and yet they are reckoned religious people. Surely it cannot be wrong. All this is very puzzling. What is he to do?

He is tried by questions about reading. He does not wish to read what is really bad, and has not time for much reading beside the Bible. Ought he, or ought he not, to read such things as skeptical writings, or French novels, or semi – popish poetry? Can there really be much harm in it? Do not many persons, as good as himself, read these things? And after all, the Bible has not expressly forbidden Emerson or Eugene Sue. All this is very puzzling. What is he to do?

There is only one answer to all these questions. A man must make the Bible his rule of conduct. He must make its leading principles the compass by which he steers his course through life. By the letter or spirit of the Bible he must test every difficult point and question. To the law and to the testimony! What saith the Scripture? He ought to care nothing for what other people may think right. He ought not to set his watch by the clock of his neighbor, but by the sun – dial of the word.

Reader, I charge you solemnly to act on the maxim I have just laid down, and to adhere to it rigidly all the days of your life. You will never repent of it. Make it a leading principle never to act contrary to the word. Care not for the charge of over – strictness, and needless precision. Remember, you serve a strict and holy God. Listen not to the common objection, that the rule you have laid down is impossible, and cannot be observed in such a world as this. Let those who make such an objection speak out plainly, and tell us for what the Bible was given to man. Let them remember that by the Bible we shall all be judged at the last day, and let them learn to judge themselves by it here, lest they be judged and condemned by it hereafter. Reader, this mighty rule of faith and practice is the book about which I am addressing you this day. Surely it is no light matter what you are doing with the Bible. Surely when danger is abroad on the right hand and on the left, you should consider what you are doing with the safe – guard which God has provided. I charge you, I beseech you, to give an honest answer to my question. What are you doing with the Bible? – Do you read it? HOW READEST THOU?

VIII. I ask in the next place, because the Bible is Hie book which all true servants of God have always lived on and loved.

Every living thing which God creates requires food. The life that God imparts needs sustaining and nourishing. It is so with animal and vegetable life, – with birds, beasts, fishes, reptiles, insects, and plants. It is equally so with spiritual life. When the Holy Ghost raises a man from the death of sin, and makes him a new creature in Christ Jesus, the new principle in that man's heart requires food, and the only food which will sustain it is the word of God.

There never was a man or woman converted, from one end of the world to the other, who did not love the revealed will of God. Just as a child born into the world desires naturally the milk provided for its nourishment, so does a soul born again desire the sincere milk of the word. This is a common mark of all the children of God, – they delight in the law of the Lord.

Show me a person who despises Bible reading, or thinks little of Bible preaching, and I hold it to be a certain fact that he is not yet born again. He may be zealous about forms and ceremonies. He may be diligent in attending sacraments and daily services. But if these things are more precious to him than the Bible, I cannot think he is a converted man. Tell me what the Bible is to a man, and I will generally tell you what he is. This is the pulse to try, – this is the barometer to look at, – if we would know the state of the heart. I have no notion of the Spirit dwelling in a man, and not giving clear evidence of His presence. And I believe it to be a signal evidence of the Spirit's presence, when the word is really precious to a man's soul.

Love to the word is one of the characteristics we see in Job. Little as we know of this Patriarch and his age, this at least stands out clearly. He says, "I have esteemed the words of his mouth more than my necessary food." (Job, xxiii. 12.)

Love to the word is a shining feature in the character of David. Mark how it appears all through that wonderful part of Scripture, the cxixth Psalm. He might well say, "Oh! how I love thy law."

Love to the word is a striking point in the character of St. Paul. What were he and his companions but men mighty in the Scriptures? What were his sermons but expositions and applications of the word?

Love to the word appears pre – eminently in our Lord and Saviour Jesus Christ. He read it publicly. He quoted it continually. He expounded it frequently. He advised the Jews to search it. He used it as His weapon to resist the devil. He said repeatedly "The Scripture must be fulfilled." – Almost the last thing He did was to open the understanding of His disciples, that they might understand the Scriptures. Ah! reader, that man can be no true servant of Christ, who has not something of his Master's mind and feeling toward the Bible.

Love to the word has been a prominent feature in the history of all the saints, of whom we know anything, since the days of the apostles. This is the lamp which Athanasius, and Chrysostom, and Augustine followed. This is the compass which kept the Vallenses and Albigenses from making shipwreck of the faith. This is the well which was re – opened by Wycliffe and Luther, after it had been long stopped up. This is the sword with which Latimer, and Jewell, and Knox won their victories. This is the manna which fed Baxter, and Owen, and the noble host of the Puritans, and made them strong to battle. This is the armory from which Whitefield and Wesley drew their powerful weapons. This is the mine from which Bickersteth and M'Cheyne brought forth rich gold. Differing as these holy men did in some matters, on one point they were all agreed, – they all delighted in the word.

Love to the word is one of the first things that appears in the converted heathen, at the various Missionary stations throughout the world. In hot climates and in cold, – among savage people and among civilized, – in New Zealand, in the South Sea Islands, in Africa, in Hindostan, – it is always the same. They enjoy hearing it read. They long to be able to read it themselves. They wonder why Christians did not send it to them before. How striking is the picture which Moff at draws of Africaner, the fierce South African chieftain, when first brought under the power of the Gospel!" Often have I seen him," he says, "under the shadow of a great rock nearly the live – long day, eagerly perusing the pages of the Bible." How touching is the expression of a poor converted negro, speaking of the Bible! He said, "It is never old and never cold." How affecting was the language of another old Negro, when some would have dissuaded him from learning to read, because of his great age.

"No!" he said, "I will never give it up till I die. It is worth all the labor to be able to read that one verse, 'God so loved the world, that he gave his only begotten Son, that whosoever believeth in him should not perish, but have eternal life."

Love to the Bible is one of the grand points of agreement among all converted men and women in our own land. Episcopalians and Presbyterians, Baptists and Independents, Methodists and Plymouth Brethren, – all unite in honoring the Bible, as soon as they are real Christians. This is the manna which all the tribes of our Israel feed upon, and find satisfying food. This is the fountain round which all the various portions of Christ's flock meet together, and from which no sheep goes thirsty away. Oh! that believers in this country would learn to cleave more closely to the written word! Oh! that they would see that the more the Bible, and the Bible only, is the substance of men's religion, the more they agree! It is probable there never was an uninspired book more universally admired than Bunyan's Pilgrim's Progress. It is a book which all denominations of Christians delight to honor. It has won praise from all parties. Now what a striking fact it is, that the author was pre – eminently a man of one book! He had read hardly anything but the Bible.

Away with the foolish idea, that making the Bible alone the rule of faith hinders unity, and that those who profess to glory in the Bible, and nothing but the Bible, are hopelessly divided! It is a weak invention of the enemy. It is a base calumny. No doubt there is much dissension and party spirit among mere outward professors; but among the great bulk of believing Protestants there is a wonderful amount of unity, – real, thorough, and deep, far deeper than the boasted unity of Borne. Their differences are merely about the outward trappings of Christianity. About the body of the faith they are all agreed. Their differences are studiously exaggerated by the enemies of true religion. Their points of agreement, – such as the "Harmony of Protestant Confessions" exhibits, are studiously kept out of sight. Their differences are differences which in times of common danger are soon forgotten. Their unity is an unity which in front of sin, heathenism, and persecution, stands boldly out. Ridley and Hooper forgot their old disagreements when they found themselves in Queen Mary's prisons. Churchmen and Nonconformists laid aside their quarrels when James II tried to bring back Popery to England. Protestant missionaries, of different denominations, find they can work and pray together, when they are in the midst of idolaters. Protestant believers in London have proved to the world that they can agree to labor together for the conversion of souls, by maintaining that glorious Institution, the London City Mission. And what is the secret of all this deep – seated unity? It comes from this, – that all believers on earth are not only born of one Spirit, but also read one holy book, and feed on the bread of one Bible.

Ah! reader, it is a blessed thought that there will be "much people" in heaven at last. Few as the Lord's people undoubtedly are at any one given time or place, yet all gathered together at last, they will be "a multitude that no man can number." They will be of one heart and mind. They will have passed through like experience. They will all have repented, believed, lived holy, prayerful, and humble. They will all have washed their robes and made them white in the blood of the Lamb. But one thing beside all this they will have in common. They will all love the texts and doctrines of the Bible. The Bible will have been their food and delight, in the days of their pilgrimage on earth. And the Bible will be a common subject of joyful meditation and retrospect, when they are gathered together in heaven.

Reader, this book, which all true Christians live upon and love, is the subject about which I am addressing you this day. Surely it is no light matter what you are doing with the Bible. Surely it is a matter for serious inquiry, whether you know anything of this love to the word, and have this mark of walking in the footsteps of the flock. I charge you, I entreat you to give me an honest answer. What are you doing with the Bible? Do you read it? HOW READEST THOU?

IX. I ask, in the last place, because the Bible is the only book which can comfort a man in the last hours of his life.

Death is an event which in all probability is before us all. There is no avoiding it. It is the river which each of us must cross. I who write, and you who read, have each one day to die. It is good to remember this. We are all sadly apt to put away the subject from us. "Each man thinks each man mortal but himself." I want every one to do his duty in life, but I also want every one to think of death. I want every one to know how to live, but I also want every one to know how to die.

Death is a solemn event to all. It is the winding up of all earthly plans and expectations. It is a separation from all we have loved and lived with. It is often accompanied by much bodily pain and distress. It brings us to the grave, the worm, and corruption. It opens the door to judgment and eternity, – to heaven or to hell. It is an event after which there is no change, or space for repentance. Other mistakes may be corrected or retrieved, but not a mistake on our death – beds. As the tree falls, there it must lie. No conversion in the coffin! No new birth after we have ceased to breathe! And death is before us all. It may be close at hand. The time of our departure is quite uncertain. But sooner or later we must each lie down alone and die. All these are serious considerations.

Death is a solemn event, even to the believer in Christ. For him no doubt the sting of death is taken away. Death has become one of his privileges, for he is Christ's. Living or dying, he is the Lord's. If he lives, Christ lives in him, and if he dies, he goes to live with Christ. To him to live is Christ, and to die is gain. Death frees him from many trials, – from a weak body, a corrupt heart, a tempting devil, and an ensnaring or persecuting world. Death admits him to the enjoyment of many blessings. He rests from his labors: – The hope of a joyful resurrection is changed into a certainty: – He has the company of holy redeemed spirits: – He is with Christ. All this is true, – and yet, even to a believer, death is a solemn thing. Flesh and blood naturally shrinks from it. To part from all we love is a wrench and trial to the feelings. The world we go to is a world unknown, even though it is our home. Friendly and harmless as death is to a believer, it is not an event to be treated lightly. It always must be a very solemn thing.

Reader, it becomes every one to consider calmly how he is going to meet death. Gird up your loins, like a man, and look the subject in the face. Listen to me, while I tell you a few things about the end we are coming to. The good things of the world cannot comfort a man when he draws near death. All the gold of California and Australia will not provide light for the dark valley. Money can buy the best medical advice and attendance for a man's body. But money cannot buy peace for his conscience, heart, and soul.

Relations, loved friends, and servants cannot comfort a man when he draws near death. They may minister affectionately to his bodily wants. They may watch by his bed – side tenderly, and anticipate his every wish. They may smooth down his dying pillow, and support his sinking frame in their arms. But they cannot "minister to a mind diseased." They cannot stop the achings of a troubled heart. They cannot screen an uneasy conscience from the eye of God.

The pleasures of the world cannot comfort a man when he draws near death. The brilliant ball – room, – the merry dance, – the midnight revel, – the party to Epsom races, – the card table, – the box at the opera, – the voices of singing men and singing women, – all these are at length distasteful things. To hear of hunting and shooting engagements gives him no pleasure. To be invited to feasts, and regattas, and fancy – fairs, gives him no ease. He cannot hide from himself that these are hollow, empty, powerless things. They jar upon the ear of his conscience. They are out of harmony with his condition. They cannot stop one gap in his heart, when the last enemy is coming in like a flood. They cannot make him calm in the prospect of meeting a holy God.

Books and newspapers cannot comfort a man when he draws near death. The most brilliant writings of Macaulay or Dickens will pall upon his ear. The most splendid article in the Times will fail to interest them. The Edinburgh and Quarterly Reviews will give him no pleasure. Punch and the Illustrated News, and the last new novel, will lie unopened and unheeded. Their time will be past. Their vocation will be gone. Whatever they may be in health, they are useless in the hour of death.

There is but one fountain of comfort for a man drawing near to his end, and that is the Bible. Chapters out of the Bible, – texts out of the Bible, – statements of truth taken out of the Bible, – books containing matter drawn from the Bible, – these are a man's only chance of comfort, when he comes to die. I do not at all say that the Bible will do good, as a matter of course, to a dying man, if he has not valued it before. I know, unhappily, too much of death – beds to say that. I do not say whether it is probable that he who has been unbelieving and neglectful of the Bible in life, will at once believe and get comfort from it in death. But I do say, positively, that no dying man will ever get real comfort, except from the contents of the word of God. All comfort from any other source is a house built upon sand.

I lay this down as a rule of universal application. I make no exception in favor of any class on earth. Kings and poor men, learned and unlearned, – all are on a level in this matter. There is not a jot of real consolation for any dying man, unless he gets it from the Bible. Chapters, passages, texts, promises, and doctrines of Scripture, – heard, received, believed, and rested on, – these are the only comforters I dare promise to any one, when he leaves the world. Taking the sacrament will do a man no more good than the Popish extreme unction, so long as the word is not received and believed. Priestly absolution will no more ease the conscience than the incantations of a heathen magician, if the poor dying sinner does not receive and believe Bible truth.

I tell every one who reads this tract, that although men may seem to get on comfortably without the Bible while they live, they may be sure that without the Bible they cannot comfortably die. It was a true confession of the learned Selden, "There is no book upon which we can rest in a dying moment but the Bible."

I might easily confirm all I have just said by examples and illustrations. I might show you the death – beds of men who have affected to despise the Bible. I might tell you how Voltaire and Paine, the famous infidels, died in misery, bitterness, rage, fear, and despair. I might show you the happy death – beds of those who have loved the Bible and believed it, and the blessed effect the sight of their death – beds had on others. Cecil, a minister whose praise ought to be in all churches, says,

"I shall never forget standing by the bed – side of my dying mother. 'Are you afraid to die?' I asked. 'No!' she replied. 'But why does the uncertainty of another state give you no concern?' 'Because God has said, ' Fear not; when thou passest through the waters I will be with thee, and through the rivers, they shall not overflow thee.'"

I might easily multiply illustrations of this kind. But I think it better to conclude this part of my subject, by giving the result of my own observation as a minister.

I have seen not a few dying persons in my time. I have seen great varieties of manner and deportment among them. I have seen some die sullen, silent, and comfortless. I have seen others die ignorant, unconcerned, and apparently without much fear. I have seen some die so wearied out with long illness, that they were quite willing to depart, and yet they did not seem to me at all in a fit state to go before God. I have seen others die with professions of hope and trust in God, without leaving satisfactory evidences that they were on the rock. I have seen others die, who I believe were in Christ, and safe, and yet they never seemed to enjoy much sensible comfort. I have seen some few dying in the full assurance of hope, and like Bunyan's "Standfast," giving glorious testimony to Christ's faithfulness, even in the river. But one thing I have never seen. I never saw any one enjoy what I should call real, solid, calm, reasonable peace on his death – bed, who did not draw his peace from the Bible. And this I am bold to say, that the man who thinks to go to his death – bed without having the Bible for his comforter, his companion, and his friend, is one of the greatest madmen in the world. There are no comforts for the soul but Bible comforts, and he who has not got hold of these, has got hold of nothing at all, unless it be a broken reed.

Reader, the only comforter for a death – bed is the book about which I address you this day. Surely it is no light matter whether you read that book or not. Surely a dying man, in a dying world, should seriously consider whether he has got anything to comfort him, when his turn comes to die. I charge you, I entreat you, for the last time, to give an honest answer to my question. What are you doing with the Bible? – Do you read it? HOW READEST THOU?

X. A Warning To Those Who Chose Not To Read The Bible

Reader, I have now given you the reason why I ask you a question about the Bible. I have shown you that knowledge of the Bible is absolutely necessary to salvation, – that no book is written in such a manner as the Bible, that no book contains such matter, – that no book has done so much for the world generally, – that no book can do so much for every one who reads it aright, – that no book is so awfully neglected, – that this book is the only rule of faith and practice, – that it is, and always has been, the food of all true servants of God, – and that it is the only book, which can comfort men when they die. All these are ancient things. I do not pretend to tell you anything new. I have only gathered together old truths, and tried to mould them into a new shape. Let me finish all, by addressing a few plain words to the conscience of every class of readers.

This tract may fall into the hands of some who can read, but never do read the Bible at all. Reader, are you one of them? If you are, I have something to say to you.

I cannot comfort you in your present state of mind. It would be mockery and deceit to do so. I cannot speak to you of peace and heaven, while you treat the Bible as you do. You are in danger of losing your soul.

You are in danger, because your neglected Bible is a plain evidence that you do not love God. The health of a man's body may generally be known by his appetite. The health of a man's soul may be known by his treatment of the Bible. Now you are manifestly laboring under a sore disease. Reader, will you not repent?

You are in danger, because God will reckon with you for your neglect of the Bible in the day of judgment. You will have to give account of your use of time, strength, and money; and you will also have to give account of your use of the word. You will not stand at that bar side by side with the Patagonian, who never heard of the Bible. To whom much is given, of them much will be required. Of all men's buried talents, none will weigh them down so heavily as a neglected Bible. As you deal with the Bible, so God will deal with your soul. Reader, I say again, will you not repent? You are in danger, because there is no degree of error in religion into which you may not fall. You are at the mercy of the first clever Jesuit, Mormonite, Socinian, Turk, or Jew, who may happen to .meet you. A land of unwalled villages is not more defenceless against an enemy, than a man who neglects his Bible. You may go on tumbling from one step of delusion to another, till at length you are landed in the pit of hell. Reader, I say once more, will you not repent?

You are in danger, because there is not a single reasonable excuse you can allege for neglecting the Bible. You have no time to read it forsooth! But you can make time for eating, drinking, sleeping, and perhaps for newspaper reading and smoking. You might easily make time to read the word. Alas! it is not want of time, but waste of time that ruins souls. You find it too troublesome to read forsooth! You had better say at once it is too much trouble to go to heaven, and you are content to go to hell. Truly these excuses are like the rubbish round the walls of Jerusalem in Nehemiah's days. They would all soon disappear if, like the Jews, you had "a mind to work." Reader, I say for the last time, will you not repent?

I know I cannot reach your heart. I cannot make you see and feel these things. I can only enter my solemn protest against your present treatment of the Bible, and lay that protest before your conscience. I do so with all my soul. Oh! beware lest you repent too late! Beware lest you put off seeking for the Bible till you send for the doctor in your last illness, and then find the Bible a sealed book, and dark as the cloud between the hosts of Israel and Egypt, to your anxious soul! Beware lest you go on saying all your life, "Men do very well without all this Bible reading," and find at length, to your cost, that men do very ill, and end in hell! Beware lest the day come, when you will feel, "Had I but honored the Bible as much as I have honored the newspaper, I should not have been left without comfort in my last hours!" Bible neglecting reader, I give you a plain warning. The plague – cross is at present on your door. The Lord have mercy upon your soul!

XI. Practical Advice For Reading The Bible

This tract may fall into the hands of someone who is willing to begin reading the Bible, but wants advice on the subject. Reader, are you that man? Listen to me, and I will give you a few short hints.

For one thing, begin reading your Bible this very day. 'The way to do a thing is to do it, and the way to read the Bible is actually to read it. It is not meaning, or wishing, or resolving, or intending, or thinking about it, which will advance you one step. You must positively read. There is no royal road in this matter, any more than in the matter of prayer. If you cannot read yourself, you must persuade somebody else to read to you. But one way or another, through eyes or ears, the words of Scriptures must actually pass before your mind.

For another thing, read the Bible with an earnest desire to understand it. Think not for a moment that the great object is to turn over a certain quantity of printed paper, and that it matters nothing whether you understand it or not. Some ignorant people seem to fancy that all is done, if they clear off so many chapters every day, though they may not have a notion what they are all about, and only know that they have pushed on their mark so many leaves. This is turning Bible reading into a mere form. It is almost as bad as the Popish habit of buying indulgences, by saying a fabulous number of ave – marias and paternosters. It reminds one – of the poor Hottentot, who ate up a Dutch hymn – book, because he saw it comforted his neighbors' hearts. Settle it down in your mind, as a general principle, that a Bible not understood is a Bible that does no good. Say to yourself often as you read, "What is all this about?" Dig for the meaning, like a man digging for Australian gold. Work hard, and do not give up the work in a hurry.

For another thing, read the Bible with deep reverence. Say to your soul, whenever you open the Bible, "0 my soul, thou art going to read a message from God." The sentences of judges, and the speeches of kings, are received with awe and respect. How much more reverence is due to the words of the Judge of judges, and King of kings! Avoid, as you would cursing and swearing, that irreverent habit of mind, which some German divines have unhappily taken up about the Bible. They handle the contents of the holy book as carelessly and disrespectfully, as if the writers were such men as themselves. They make one think of a child composing a book to expose the fancied ignorance of his own father, – or of a pardoned murderer criticising the hand – writing and style of his own reprieve. Enter rather into the spirit of Moses on Mount Horeb: "Put thy shoes from off thy feet; the place whereon thou standest is holy ground."

For another thing, read the Bible with earnest prayer for the teaching and help 'of the Holy Spirit. Here is the rock on which many make shipwreck at the very outset. They do not ask for wisdom and instruction, and so they find the Bible dark, and carry nothing away from it. You should pray for the Spirit to guide you into all truth. You should beg the Lord Jesus Christ to open your understanding, as He did that of His disciples. The Lord God, by whose inspiration the book was written, keeps the keys of the book, and alone can enable you to understand it profitably. Nine times over in one Psalm does David cry, "Teach me." Five times over, in the same Psalm, does he say, "Give me understanding." Well says Owen.

"There is a sacred light in the word: but there is a covering and veil on the eyes of men, so that they cannot behold it aright. Now the removal of this veil is the peculiar work of the Holy Spirit."

Humble prayer will throw more light on your Bible, than Poole's Synopsis, or all the commentaries that ever were written. Remember this, and say always, "O God, for Christ's sake, give me the teaching of the Spirit."

For another thing, read the Bible with childlike faith and humanity. Open your heart as you open your book, and say, "Speak Lord, for thy servant heareth." Resolve to believe implicitly whatever you find there, however much it may run counter to your own prejudices. Resolve to receive heartily every statement of truth, whether you like it or not. Beware of that miserable habit of mind into which some readers of the Bible fall. They receive some doctrines, because they like them. They reject others, because they are condemning to themselves, or to some lover, or relation, or friend. At this rate the Bible is useless. Are we to be judges of what ought to be in the word? Do we know better than God? Settle it down in your mind that you will receive all, and believe all, and that what you cannot understand you will take on trust. Remember, when you pray, you are speaking to God, and God hears you. But, remember, when you read, God is speaking to you, and you are not to answer again, but to listen.

For another thing, read the Bible in a spirit of obedience and self – application. Sit down to the study of it with a daily determination that you will live by its rules, rest on its statements, and act on its commands. Consider, as you travel through every chapter, "How does this affect my position and course of conduct? What does this teach me?" It is poor work to read the Bible for mere curiosity and speculative purposes, in order to fill your head and store your mind with opinions, while you do not allow the book to influence your heart and life. That Bible is read best which is practised most.

For another thing, read the Bible daily. Make it a part of every day's business to read and meditate on some portion of God's work. Private means of grace are just as needful every day for our souls, as food and clothing for our bodies. Yesterday's bread will not feed the laborer to – day, and to – day's bread will not feed the laborer to – morrow. Do as the Israelites did in the wilderness. Gather your manna fresh every morning. Choose your own seasons and hours. Do not scramble over and hurry your reading. Give your Bible the best, and not the worst part of your time. But whatever plan you pursue, let it be a rule of your life to visit the throne of grace and the Bible every day.

For another thing, read all the Bible, and read it in an orderly way. I fear there are many parts of the word which some people never read at all. This is, to say the least, a very presumptuous habit. All Scripture is profitable. To this habit may be traced the want of broad, well – proportioned views of truth, which is so common. Some people's Bible – reading is a system of perpetual dipping and picking. They do not seem to have an idea of regularly going through the whole book. This also is a great mistake. No doubt in time of sickness and affliction it is allowable to search out seasonable portions. But with this exception, I believe it is by far the best plan to begin the Old and New Testaments at the same time, – read each straight through to the end, and then begin again. This is a matter in which every one must be persuaded in his own mind. I can only say it has been my own plan for fifteen years, and I have never seen cause to alter it.

For another thing, read the Bible fairly and honestly. Determine to take everything in its plain, obvious meaning, and regard all forced interpretations with great suspicion.

As a general rule, whatever a verse of the Bible seems to mean, it does mean. Cecil's rule is a very valuable one: – " The right way of interpreting Scripture is to take it as we find it, without any attempt to force it into any particular system." Well said Hooker, "I hold it as a most infallible rule in the exposition of Scripture, that when a literal construction will stand, the furthest from the literal is commonly the worst."

In the last place, read the Bible with Christ continually in view. The grand primary object of all Scripture is to testify of Jesus. Old Testament ceremonies are shadows of Christ. Old Testament judges and deliverers are types of Christ. Old Testament history shows the world's need of Christ. Old Testament prophecies are full of Christ's sufferings, and of Christ's glory yet to come. The first advent and the second, – the Lord's humiliation and the Lord's kingdom, – the cross and the crown, shine forth everywhere in the Bible. Keep fast hold on this clue, if you would read the Bible aright.

Reader, I might easily add to these hints, if time permitted. Few and short as they are, you will find them worth attention. Act upon them, and I firmly believe you will never be allowed to miss the way to heaven. Act upon them, and you will find light continually increasing in your mind. No book of evidence can be compared with that internal evidence which he obtains, who daily uses the word in the right way. Such a man does not need the books of learned men, like Paley, and Wilson, and M'Ilvaine. He has the witness in himself. The book satisfies and feeds his soul. A poor Christian woman once said to an infidel,

"I am no scholar. I cannot argue like you. But I know that honey is honey, because it leaves a sweet taste in my mouth. And I know the Bible to be God's book, because of the taste it leaves in my heart."

This tract may fall into the hands of someone who loves and believes the Bible, and yet reads it but little. I fear there are many such in this day. It is a day of bustle and hurry. It is a day of talking, and committee meetings, and public work. These things are all very well in their way, but I fear that sometimes they clip and cut short private reading of the Bible. Reader, does your conscience tell you that you are one of the persons I speak of? Listen to me, and I will say a few things which deserve your serious attention.

You are the man that is likely to get little comfort from the Bible in time of need. Trial is a striking season. Affliction is a searching wind, which strips the leaves off the trees, and brings to light the birds' nests. Now I fear that your stores of Bible consolations may one day run very low. I fear lest you should find yourself at last on very short allowance, and come into harbor weak, worn, and thin.

You are the man that is likely never to be established in the truth I shall not be surprised to hear that you are troubled with doubts and questionings about assurance, grace, faith, perseverance, and the like. The devil is an old and cunning enemy. Like the Benjamites, he can throw stones at a hair – breadth, and not miss. He can quote Scripture readily enough when he pleases. Now you are not sufficiently ready with your weapons to be able to fight a good fight with him. Your armor does not fit you well. Your sword sits loosely in your hand.

You are the man that is likely to make mistakes in life. I shall not wonder if I am told that you have erred about your own marriage, – erred about your children's education, – erred about the conduct of your household, erred about the company you keep. The world you steer through is full of rocks, and shoals, and sand – banks. You are not sufficiently familiar either with the lights or charts.

You are the man that is likely to be carried away by some specious false teacher for a season. It will not surprise me, if I hear that some one of those clever, eloquent men, who can "make the worse appear the better cause," is leading you into many follies. You are wanting in ballast. No wonder if you are tossed to and fro, like a cork on the waves.

Reader, all these are uncomfortable things. I want you to escape them all. Take the advice I offer you this day. Do not merely read your Bible a little, but read it a great deal. Let the word of Christ dwell in you richly. Do not be a mere babe in spiritual knowledge. Seek to become well – instructed in the kingdom of heaven, and to be continually adding new things to old. A religion of feeling is an uncertain thing. It is like the tide, sometimes high, and sometimes low. It is like the moon, sometimes bright and sometimes dim. A religion of deep Bible knowledge, is a firm and lasting possession. It enables a man not merely to say, "I feel hope in Christ," – but, "I know whom I have believed."

This tract may fall into the hands of some one who reads the Bible much, and yet fancies he is no better for his reading. This is a crafty temptation of the devil. At one stage he says, "Do not read the Bible at all." At another he says, "Your reading does you no good: give it up." Reader, are you that man? I feel for you from the bottom of my soul. Let me try to do you good.

Do not think you are getting no good from the Bible, merely because you do not see that good day by day. The greatest effects are by no means those which make the most noise, and are most easily observed. The greatest defects are often silent, quiet, and hard to detect at the time they are being produced. Think of the influence of the moon upon the earth, and of the air upon the human lungs. Remember how silently the dew falls, and how imperceptibly the grass grows. There may be far more doing than you think in your soul by your Bible – reading.

The word may be gradually producing deep impressions on your heart, of which you are not at present aware. Often when the memory is retaining no facts, the character of a man is receiving some everlasting impression. Is sin becoming every year more hateful to you? Is Christ becoming every year more precious? Is holiness becoming every year more lovely and desirable in your eyes? If these things are so, take courage. The Bible is doing you good, though you may not be able to trace it out day by day.

The Bible may be restraining you from some sin or delusion, into which you would otherwise run. It may be daily keeping you back, and hedging you up, and preventing many a false step. Ah! reader, you might soon find this out to your cost, if you were to cease reading the word. The very familiarity of blessings sometimes makes us insensible to their value. Resist the devil. Settle it down in your mind as an established rule, that whether you feel it at the moment or not, you are inhaling spiritual health by reading the Bible, and insensibly becoming more strong.

There may be some into whose hands this tract will fall who really love the Bible, live upon the Bible, and read it much. Reader, are you one of these? Give me your attention, and I will mention a few things, which we shall do well to lay to heart.

Let us resolve to read the Bible more and more every year we live. Let us try to get it rooted in our memories, and engrafted into our hearts. Let us be thoroughly well provisioned with it against the voyage of death. Who knows but we may have a very stormy passage? Sight and hearing may fail us, and we may be in deep waters. Oh! to have the word hid in our hearts in such an hour as that!

Let us resolve to be more watchful over our Bible – reading every year that we live. Let us be jealously careful about the time we give to it, and the manner that time is spent. Let us beware of omitting our daily reading without sufficient cause. Let us not be gaping, and yawning, and dozing over our book, while we read. Let us read like a London merchant studying the city article in the Times, – or like a wife reading a husband's letter from a distant land. Let us be very careful that we never exalt any minister, or sermon, or book, or tract, or friend, above the word. Cursed be that book, or tract, or human counsel, which creeps in between us and the Bible, and hides the Bible from our eyes! Once more, I say, let us be very watchful. The moment we open the Bible, the devil sits down by our side. Oh! to read with a hungry spirit, and a simple desire for edification!

Let us resolve to honor the Bible more in our families. Let us read it morning and evening to our children and households, and not be ashamed to let men see that we do so. Let us not be discouraged by seeing no good arise from it. The Bible – reading in a family has kept many a one from the gaol, the workhouse, and the Gazette, if it has not kept him from hell.

Let us resolve to meditate more on the Bible. It is good to take with us two or three texts, when we go out into the world, and to turn them over and over in our minds, whenever we have a little leisure. It keeps out many vain thoughts. It clenches the nail of daily reading. It preserves our souls from stagnating and breeding corrupt things. It sanctifies and quickens our memories, and prevents their becoming like those ponds where the frogs live, but the fish die.

Let us resolve to talk more to believers about the Bible, when we meet them. Alas! the conversation of Christians, when they do meet, is often sadly unprofitable. How many frivolous, and trifling, and uncharitable things are said! Let us bring out the Bible more, and it will help to drive the devil away, and keep our hearts in tune. Oh ! that we may all strive so to walk together in this world, that Jesus may draw near, and go with us, as he went with the two disciples journeying to Emmaus!

Let us resolve to prize the Bible more. Let us not fear being idolaters of this blessed book. those who have not the

Scriptures. Let us think of them with pity and compassion, and not judge them by the standard of people who have the word.

Let us deal gently with our Irish Brother. He may do many things which fill us with horror. But he errs, not knowing the Scriptures. He has no Bible. Let us judge charitably our Italian brother. He may seem superstitious, and lazy, and indolent, and incapable of anything great or good. But he errs, not knowing the Scriptures. He has no Bible.

Let us think lovingly of all Roman Catholic laymen on the Continent. We may feel disgusted by their adoring the Holy Coat of TreVes. We may be shocked at their credulity about the Winking Picture of the Virgin at Rimini. But we must remember that men will eat mice and rats in time of famine, and we must not marvel if souls feed on trash and garbage, when priests debar them from reading the word. They err, not knowing the Scriptures, They have no Bibles.

Last of all let us resolve to live by the Bible more and more every year we live. Let us resolutely take account of all our opinions and practices, – of our habits and tempers, – of our behavior in public and in private, – in the world, and by our own firesides. Let us measure all by the Bible, and resolve, by God's help, to conform to it. Oh! that we may learn increasingly to cleanse our ways by the word!

Reader, I commend all these things to your serious and prayerful attention. I want the ministers to be Bible – reading ministers, – the congregations, Bible – reading congregations, – and the nation, a Bible – reading nation. To bring about this desirable end, I cast in my mite into God's treasury. The Lord grant that in your case it may prove not to have been in vain.

I remain
Your affectionate Friend,

J. C. Ryle